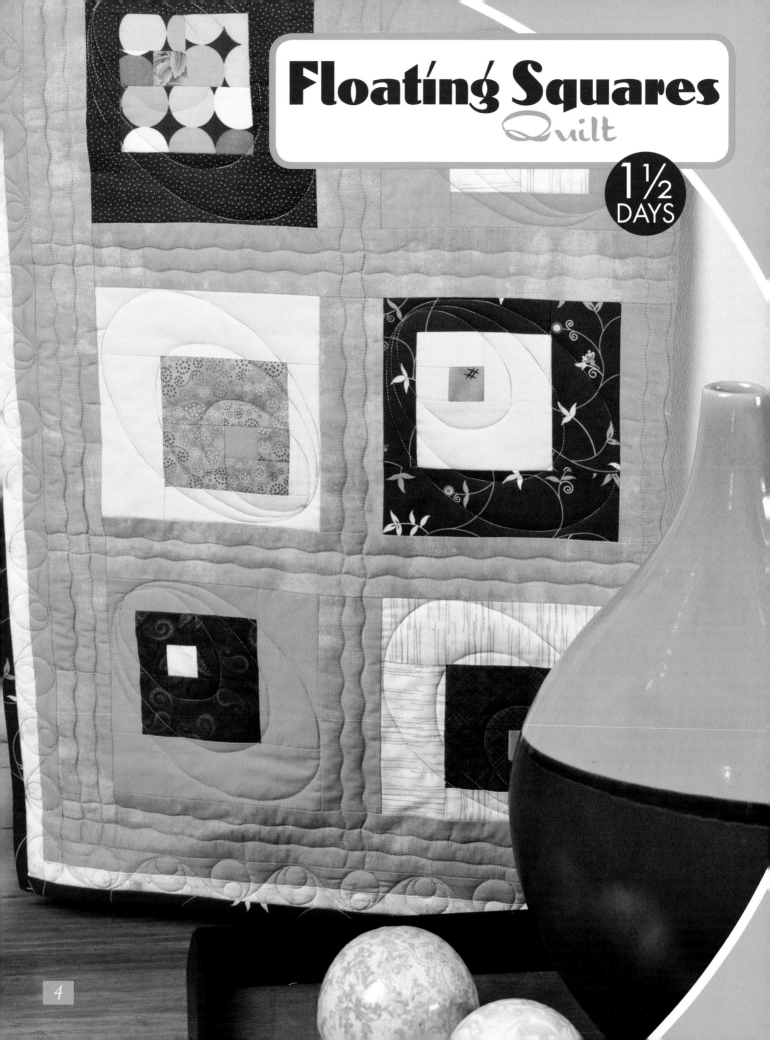

Floating Squares
Quilt

1½ DAYS

Weekend Planner

I love geometric designs because they are so handsome. Plus they are so suitable for modern decorating because the lines are "clean." The floating center square almost seems to follow you - watching your every move.

FRIDAY EVENING

Can you get off work a little early tonight to sneak off to the fabric store? It would be a fabulous way to start your weekend! Along with packing your lunch, be sure to bring your fabric requirements, quilt photo and diagram to work with you this morning. When making your fabric selections, be sure all your outside block colors show contrast to the sashing fabric. Don't worry if shopping takes you all evening, that's when you're doing all your color/fabric placement planning.

SATURDAY MORNING

Preset the coffee maker, so your favorite brew will inspire you to hop out of bed and start cutting your strips and pieces first thing. With a fresh blade for your rotary cutter, finish up the cutting task in about 1½ hours. After a scone and a second cup of Joe, get ready to do some serious stitching. So first things first, stack and organize all your block fabrics. If you can go non-stop pedal to the metal, piecing the blocks may still take about 3 hours. Have your ironing board set up right next to the sewing machine, so as you sew seams you can press and immediately go to the next step of piecing each block. This process will likely seep into your afternoon.

SATURDAY AFTERNOON

It's always better to take the occasional break than make a bunch of mistakes. Eating a little lunch will keep your blood sugar in line and keep you thinking straight.

After all your blocks are done, sigh with pride and plan for a couple more hours to piece your top and add the borders. It's been a full day of accomplishment. Clean up your mess tomorrow!

How long it will take you to accomplish tasks is an estimate and may vary greatly per individual. You may want to allow extra time for any distractions that may come up – like hunting down your seam ripper. (Happens to the best of us!)

Floating Squares Quilt Finished Size: 42" x 51"	FIRST CUT		SECOND CUT	
	Number of Strips or Pieces	Dimensions	Number of Pieces	Dimensions
See Important Tips prior to cutting.				
Block Center Assorted scraps	20	1½" squares		
Block First Border ⅛ yard each of 20 Assorted fabrics	1*	2½" x 13" *cut for each fabric	1* 1* 1* 1*	2½" x 4½" 2½" square 1½" x 2½" 1½" square
Block Outside Border ⅛ yard each of 20 Assorted fabrics	1*	2½" x 27" *cut for each fabric	1* 1* 1* 1*	2½" x 7½" 2½" x 5½" 1½" x 5½" 1½" x 4½"
Sashing** 1 yard	12	2½" x 42"	6 15	2½" x 34½" 2½" x 7½"
First Border ¼ yard	5	1¼" x 42"	2	1¼" x 38½"
Outside Border ¼ yard	5	1¼" x 42"	2	1¼" x 40"
Binding ½ yard	5	2¾" x 42"		

Backing - 2⅔ yards
Batting - 48" x 57"
**Note: Do not use same colorway as Sashing for Block Outside Border pieces.

Fabric Requirements and Cutting Instructions
Read all instructions before beginning and use ¼"-wide seam allowances throughout. Read Cutting Strips and Pieces on page 124 prior to cutting fabric.

Important Tips
Refer to Getting Started prior to selecting fabric pieces. Each block uses three different fabrics. For Block First Border, cut one of each size from one piece of fabric. For Outside Border, cut one of each size from one piece of fabric.

Getting Started

This quilt consists of four different colors in a variety of patterns and shades. Blocks in our quilt consist of four corals, three greens, four browns, and four ivories. Additional fabrics can be used to create a scrappier look, as long as fabrics are one of the four colorways. Because green was used in the Sashing, no green fabrics were used for Block Outside Border pieces. Diagram below shows the placement of fabrics we used for our quilt. Since individual fabric selections will vary from quilt to quilt, the total number of pieces used for each color is listed in chart. Block measures 7½" square (unfinished). Refer to Accurate Seam Allowance on page 124. Whenever possible use Assembly Line Method on page 124. Press seams in direction of arrows.

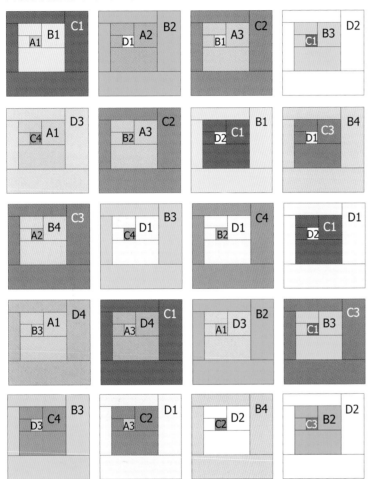

Letters indicate fabric color while numbers represent different fabric shades or texture used in quilt. A-Green, B-Coral, C-Brown & D-Ivory.

Making the Blocks

1. Sew one 1½" Block Center square to one 1½" Block First Border square as shown. Sew this unit to one matching 1½" x 2½" Block First Border piece. Press. Make twenty in assorted fabric combinations.

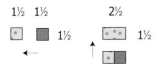

Make 20
in assorted fabric combinations

2. Sew one unit from step 1 to one matching 2½" Block First Border square as shown. Press. Sew this unit to one matching 2½" x 4½" Block First Border piece. Press. Make twenty in assorted fabric combinations.

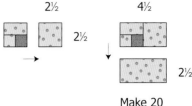

Make 20
in assorted combinations

3. Sew one unit from step 3 to one 1½" x 4½" Block Outside Border piece as shown. Press. Sew this unit to one matching 1½" x 5½" Block Outside Border piece. Press. Make twenty in assorted fabric combinations.

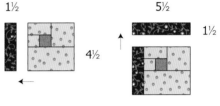

Make 20
in assorted fabric combinations

4. Sew one unit from step 3 to one matching 2½" x 5½" Block Outside Border piece as shown. Press. Sew this unit to one matching 2½" x 7½" Block Outside Border piece. Press. Make twenty in assorted fabric combinations.

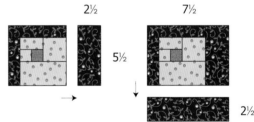

Make 20
in assorted fabric combinations
Block measures 7½" square

Tip for Aligning Blocks

Use a removable fabric marker to mark wrong side of each sashing strip as follows: 7¼", 2, 7, 2, 7, 2 and 7¼". Align these marks with seam lines, pin into position then sew rows together. After all rows have been sewn together remove markings following manufacturer's instructions.

Assembling the Quilt

1. Referring to layout, arrange and sew together four blocks from step 4 to three 2½" x 7½" Sashing pieces as shown. Press. Make five in assorted fabric combinations noting direction of blocks.

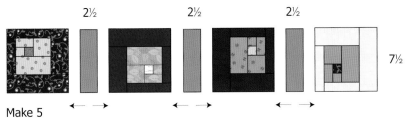

Make 5
in assorted fabric combinations

2. Referring to layout, arrange and sew together six 2½" x 34½" Sashing strips to rows from step 1. Press seams toward sashing strips. See Tip for Aligning Blocks on page 6.

3. Sew 2½" x 42" Sashing strips together end-to-end to make one continuous 2½"-wide Sashing strip. Measure quilt through center from top to bottom. Cut two 2½"-wide Sashing strips to this measurement. Sew to sides of quilt. Press seams toward sashing.

Adding the Borders

1. Refer to Adding the Borders on page 126. Sew two 1¼" x 38½" First Border strips to top and bottom of quilt. Press seams toward border.

2. Sew 1¼" x 42" First Border strips together end-to-end to make one continuous 1¼"-wide First Border strip. Measure quilt through center from top to bottom including borders just added. Cut two 1¼"-wide First Border strips to this measurement. Sew to sides of quilt. Press.

3. Sew two 1¼" x 40" Outside Border strips to top and bottom of quilt. Press. Refer to step 2 to join, measure, trim, and sew 1¼"-wide Outside Border strips to sides of quilt. Press.

Layering and Finishing

1. Cut backing crosswise into two equal pieces. Sew pieces together lengthwise to make one 48" x 80" (approximate) backing piece. Press and trim to 48" x 57".

2. Referring to Layering the Quilt on page 126, arrange and baste backing, batting, and top together. Hand or machine quilt as desired.

3. Refer to Binding the Quilt on page 126. Sew 2¾" x 42" binding strips end-to-end to make one continuous 2¾"-wide binding strip. Bind quilt to finish.

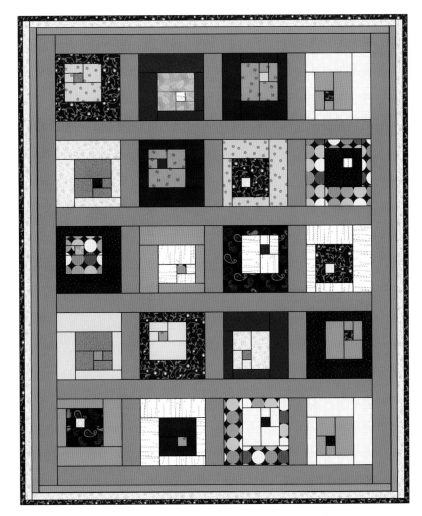

Floating Squares Quilt
42" x 51"

Floating Squares
Bed Quilt

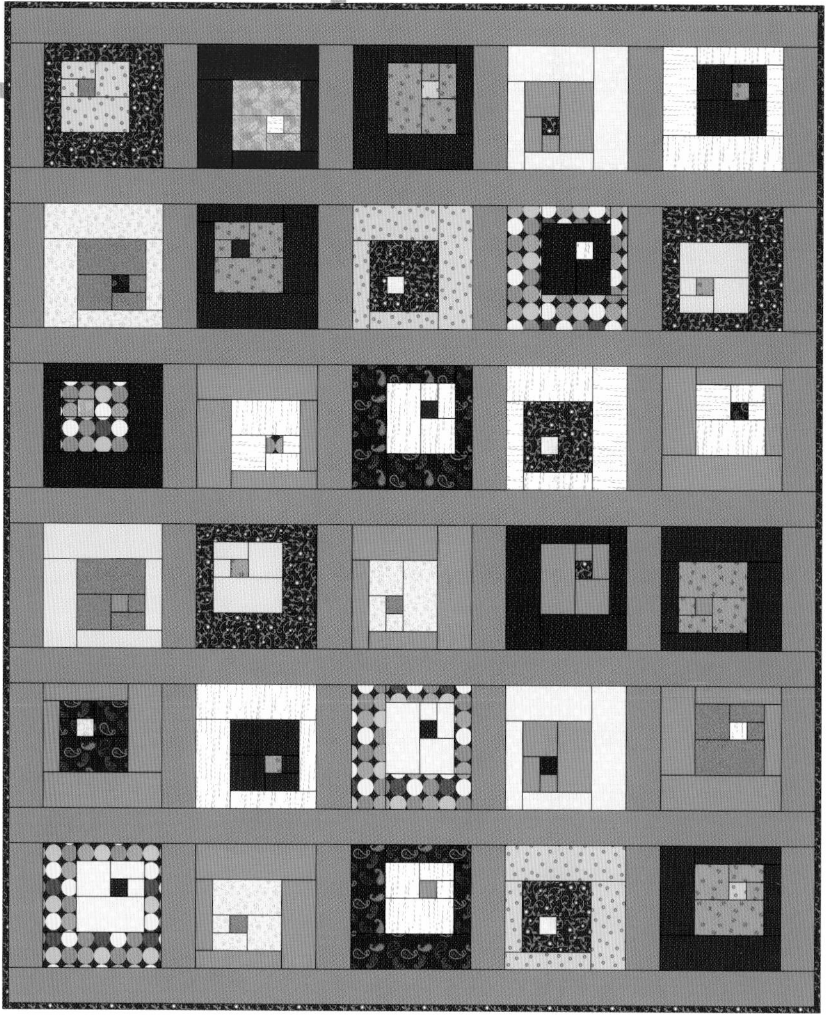

Fabric Requirements and Cutting Instructions
Read all instructions before beginning and use ¼"-wide seam allowances throughout. Read Cutting Strips and Pieces on page 124 prior to cutting fabric.

Getting Started
Simply increase the cut sizes and number of blocks to create this Floating Squares Bed Quilt. Use assorted scraps of fabrics and the same block construction and you'll have a quilt finished in no time. Block measures 11" unfinished.

Making the Quilt

1. Refer to Floating Squares Quilt on pages 4-7, Making the Quilt steps 1-4 to make thirty blocks. Note: For Block Center use 2" squares; for Block First Border use 3½" x 6½" pieces, 3½" squares, 2" x 3½" pieces, and 2" squares; and for Block Outside Border use 3½" x 11", 3½" x 8", 2" x 8", and 2" x 6½" pieces. Unfinished block measures 11" square.

2. Referring to layout, arrange six rows with six 3½" x 11" Sashing pieces and five blocks each. Sew sashing and blocks into rows noting direction of blocks. Press seams toward sashing.

3. Sew 3½" x 42" Sashing strips together end-to-end to make one continuous 3½"-wide Sashing strip. Measure rows from step 2 side to side. Cut seven 3½"-wide Sashing strips to this measurement.

4. Referring to layout, arrange sashing strips from step 3 and rows from step 2, alternating sashing and rows. Sew rows together. Press.

Layering and Finishing the Quilt

1. Cut backing crosswise into two equal pieces. Sew pieces together lengthwise to make one 80" x 93" (approximate) backing piece.

2. Referring to Layering the Quilt on page 126, arrange and baste backing, batting, and top together. Hand or machine quilt as desired.

3. Refer to Binding the Quilt on page 126. Sew 2¾" x 42" binding strips end-to-end to make one continuous 2¾"-wide binding strip. Bind quilt to finish.

Floating Squares Bed Quilt Finished Size: 71½" x 85"	FIRST CUT		SECOND CUT	
	Number of Strips or Pieces	Dimensions	Number of Pieces	Dimensions
See Important Tips prior to cutting.				
Block Center 30 Assorted scraps	30	2" squares		
Block First Border ⅛ yard each of 30 Assorted fabrics	1*	3½" x 17" *cut for each fabric	1* 1* 1* 1*	3½" x 6½" 3½" square 2" x 3½" 2" square
Block Outside Border ⅛ yard each of 30 Assorted fabrics	1*	3½" x 42" *cut for each fabric	1* 1* 1* 1*	3½" x 11" 3½" x 8" 2" x 8" 2" x 6½"
Sashing 2⅔ yards	25	3½" x 42"	36	3½" x 11"
Binding ⅞ yard	8	2¾" x 42"		
Backing - 5⅙ yards Batting - 80" x 93"				

Triple Dash
Throw Quilt

1½ DAYS

Weekend Planner

. . . .

The graphic simplicity of this design makes it particularly flexible, and should appeal to male and female alike. I did a 3-color (with a brown accent) story; however, wouldn't it also be fabulous as a scrap quilt?

FRIDAY EVENING

Dash out after work to select and purchase your fabrics. If your plan is to use this as a throw, choose a background fabric that will nicely contrast the piece of furniture that it will reside on.

SATURDAY MORNING

Don't you just love when you wake up in the morning and realize it's the weekend? Particularly when making a quilt is how you plan to spend it!

The first hour or so will be cutting all the pieces. It's all strips, which makes it easy. Get yourself (and your fabrics) organized and ready to spend the rest of the day piecing the blocks and border rows.

SATURDAY AFTERNOON

Even though the design is simple and the sewing is easy, it will still take six to seven hours to complete the blocks and checked rows. To me, that means I want to line up three movies in my DVD player. My favorites are my old Doris Day movies from the early sixties. The ones co-starring Rock Hudson are the best!

SUNDAY AFTERNOON

Yesterday was a very productive day. Give your back and shoulders a rest this morning. It's another 2½ hours of machine time to get your top all pieced together. When you're finished, ask someone for a backrub - you've earned it!

How long it will take you to accomplish tasks is an estimate and may vary greatly per individual. You may want to allow extra time for any distractions that may come up – like hunting down your seam ripper. (Happens to the best of us!)

Triple Dash Throw Quilt Finished Size: 51" x 59"	FIRST CUT		SECOND CUT	
	Number of Strips or Pieces	Dimensions	Number of Pieces	Dimensions
Fabric A Background & Outside Border 2½ yards	11	2½" x 42"	25	2½" x 6½"
	10	1½" x 42"	8	1½" x 9"
	1	1⅜" x 42"	8	1⅜" x 2"
	31	1¼" x 42"	22	1¼" x 30"
			8	1¼" x 9"
			24	1¼" x 2"
Fabric B Red Triple Dash ¼ yard each of 3 Fabrics	3*	2" x 42" *cut for each fabric	3*	2" x 30"
Fabric C Blue Triple Dash ¼ yard each of 3 Fabrics	3*	2" x 42" *cut for each fabric	3*	2" x 30"
Fabric D Green Triple Dash ¼ yard each of 3 Fabrics	3*	2" x 42" *cut for each fabric	3*	2" x 30"
Fabric E Accent Squares ⅙ yard each of 3 Fabrics	2*	2" x 42" *cut for each fabric	2*	2" x 30"
Fabric F Accent Strip ½ yard	10	1" x 42"	8	1" x 9"
Binding ⅝ yard	6	2¾" x 42"		
Backing - 3⅙ yards Batting - 57" x 65"				

Fabric Requirements and Cutting Instructions

Read all instructions before beginning and use ¼"-wide seam allowances throughout. Read Cutting Strips and Pieces on page 124 prior to cutting fabric.

Getting Started

Triple Dash blocks never looked so fine and they're simple to make using strip piecing. Block measures 6½" square (unfinished). Refer to Accurate Seam Allowance on page 124. Whenever possible use Assembly Line Method on page 124. Press seams in direction of arrows.

Making the Triple Dash Blocks

1. Arrange and sew together lengthwise three matching 2" x 30" Fabric B strips and two 1¼" x 30" Fabric A strips as shown to make a strip set. Make three, one of each combination.

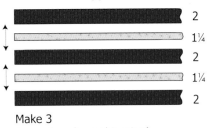

Make 3
(one of each combination)

2. A total of ten assorted segments will be needed for this quilt. Cut one strip set into four 6½"-wide segments and cut two different strip sets each into three 6½"-wide segments as shown. Block measures 6½" square.

Cut 3 or 4 segments

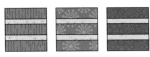

Make 10
(three of two fabric combinations & four of another fabric combination)

3. Using 2" x 30" Fabric C strips and referring to steps 1 and 2, sew and cut ten segments; three of two fabric combinations and four segments of another fabric combination. Block measures 6½" square.

Make 10
(three of two fabric combinations & four of another fabric combination)

4. Using 2" x 30" Fabric D strips and referring to steps 1 and 2, sew and cut ten segments; three of two fabric combinations and four segments of another fabric combination. Block measures 6½" square.

Make 10
(three of two fabric combinations & four of another fabric combination)

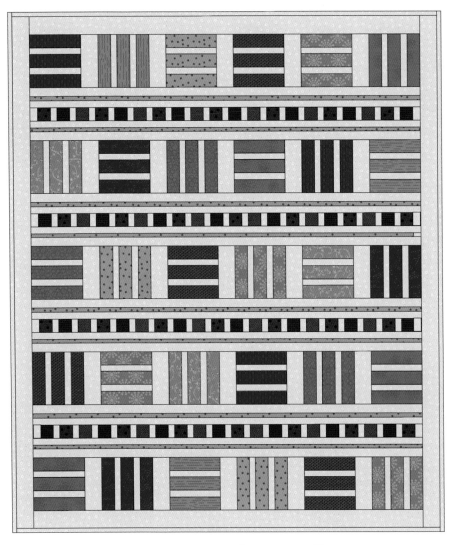

Triple Dash Throw Quilt
51" x 59"

Assembling the Quilt

1. Arrange and sew together lengthwise three different 2" x 30" Fabric E strips and two 1¼" x 30" Fabric A strips as shown to make a strip set. Make two. Cut strips into twenty-eight 2"-wide segments as shown.

Make 2
Cut 28 segments

2. Remove one Fabric E square and one Fabric A piece from four units from step 1. Arrange and sew together, two 1⅜ " x 2" Fabric A pieces, six units from step 1, six 1¼" x 2" Fabric A pieces and one unit from this step as shown. Press. Make four.

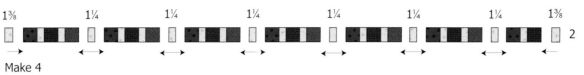

Make 4

3. Sew one 1½" x 42" and one 1½" x 9" Fabric A strips end-to-end. Press. Make eight. Repeat to sew 1¼" x 42" and 1¼" x 9" Fabric A strips end-to-end. Press. Make eight.

4. Sew one 1" x 42" and one 1" x 9" Fabric F strips end-to-end. Press. Make eight.

5. Sew lengthwise one 1"-wide Fabric F strip from step 4 between one 1½"-wide and 1¼"-wide Fabric A strips from step 3 as shown, staggering seams, to make a strip set. Press. Cut each strip set into 46½" lengths. Make eight.

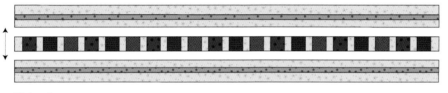

Make 8

6. Sew one unit from step 2 between two units from step 5 as shown, placing wider Fabric A strip along outside edges. Press. Make four.

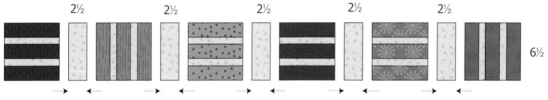

Make 4
Note: Place 1½"-wide Fabric A strips along outside edge.

7. Referring to layout on page 11 for block placement for each row, arrange and sew together two Fabric B blocks, two Fabric D blocks, two Fabric C blocks, and five 2½" x 6½" Fabric A pieces as shown. Press. Make five.

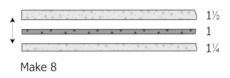

Make 5 in assorted combinations

8. Referring to layout on page 11, arrange and sew rows from step 6 and 7 together. Press.

9. Refer to Adding the Borders on page 126. Sew 2½" x 42" Fabric A strips together end-to-end to make one continuous 2½"-wide Fabric A strip. Measure quilt through center from side to side. Cut two 2½"-wide Fabric A strips to this measurement. Sew to top and bottom of quilt. Press seams toward border.

10. Measure quilt through center from top to bottom including borders just added. Cut two 2½"-wide Fabric A strips to this measurement. Sew to sides of quilt. Press.

Layering and Finishing

1. Cut backing crosswise into two equal pieces. Sew pieces together lengthwise to make one 57" x 80" (approximate) backing piece. Press and trim to 57" x 65".

2. Referring to Layering the Quilt on page 126, arrange and baste backing, batting, and top together. Hand or machine quilt as desired.

3. Refer to Binding the Quilt on page 126. Sew 2¾" x 42" binding strips end-to-end to make one continuous 2¾"-wide binding strip. Bind quilt to finish.

Cups in the Cupboard
Wallhanging

1 DAY

Weekend Planner

SATURDAY MORNING

Whether you drink tea, coffee or cocoa, a fun collection of mugs makes every morning go even better. As a quilter, it's also a blast to collect a fun assortment of fabrics. This project is a great excuse to shop through the discounted remnants or fat quarter bins to pull together an assortment of patterns and coordinates for these mug appliqués. Also, pick up your background and border fabrics as you leisurely make a morning of shopping. If you don't have matching thread colors, don't forget to pick those up too.

SATURDAY AFTERNOON

Tracing and cutting your appliqué pieces may take you a couple of hours depending on how much you like to fuss over your fabric choices. I think that fussing is a big part of the fun myself. Spend a couple more hours cutting and piecing the background. This may be a good stopping point for the afternoon. (Make a cup of cocoa as your reward.)

SUNDAY MORNING

Arrange your cups and mugs on the background and get ready to sit and appliqué. A zigzag appliqué saves tons of time versus the traditional satin stitch appliqué and it's much easier to do. Changing thread colors eats up a little more time, but it's worth it when it comes to your finished results. Two hours should be the max to complete this.

How long it will take you to accomplish tasks is an estimate and may vary greatly per individual. You may want to allow extra time for any distractions that may come up – like hunting down your seam ripper. (Happens to the best of us!)

Cups in the Cupboard Wallhanging Finished Size: 25" x 23½"	FIRST CUT		SECOND CUT	
	Number of Strips or Pieces	Dimensions	Number of Pieces	Dimensions
Fabric A Background ⅜ yard	1	6½" x 42"	1	6½" x 19½"
			1	5½" x 19½"
	1	5" x 42"	1	5" x 19½"
Fabric B Medium Accent Border ⅛ yard	3	1" x 42"	4	1" x 19½"
			2	1" x 19"
Fabric C Dark Accent Border ¼ yard	4	1½" x 42"	2	1½" x 21"
			2	1½" x 20½"
	1	1" x 42"	2	1" x 19½"
Outside Border ¼ yard	4	1½" x 42"		
Binding ⅜ yard	4	2¾" x 42"		

Appliqué Cups - Assorted scraps
Backing - ¾ yard
Batting - 29" x 27"
Lightweight Fusible Web (18"-wide) - ⅝ yard
Stabilizer (20"-wide) - ⅝ yard

Fabric Requirements and Cutting Instructions
Read all instructions before beginning and use ¼"-wide seam allowances throughout. Read Cutting Strips and Pieces on page 124 prior to cutting fabric.

Getting Started
Have a soothing cup of morning coffee relaxing in a quiet corner accented with this colorful coffee cups quilt. Refer to Accurate Seam Allowance on page 124. Press seams in direction of arrows.

Assembling the Quilt

1. Sew one 1" x 19½" Fabric B strip to one 1" x 19½" Fabric C strip as shown. Press. Make two.

19½

1
1

Make 2

2. Arrange and sew together two 1" x 19½" Fabric B strips, one 5" x 19½" Fabric A strip, two units from step 1, one 5½" x 19½" Fabric A strip, and one 6½" x 19½" Fabric A strip as shown. Press.

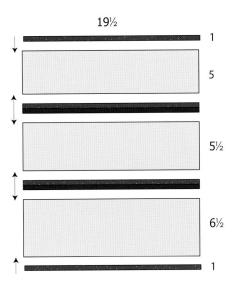

19½

1

5

5½

6½

1

3. Sew two 1" x 19" Fabric B strips to sides of unit from step 2. Press seams toward Fabric B.

4. Sew two 1½" x 20½" Fabric C strips to top and bottom of quilt. Press seams toward border just sewn. Sew two 1½" x 21" Fabric C strips to side of quilt. Press.

5. Refer to Mitered Borders on page 126. Sew 1½" x 42" Outside Border strips to top, bottom, and sides of quilt, mitering corners. Press seams toward Outside Border.

Cups in the Cupboard
Wallhanging 25" x 23½"

Adding the Appliqués

Refer to appliqué instructions on page 125. Our instructions are for Quick-Fuse Appliqué, but if you prefer hand appliqué, reverse patterns and add ¼"-wide seam allowances.

1. Some coffee cups are traced as a whole pattern piece while others are traced with a contrasting handle piece. Refer to pattern for quantity needed for each cup. Use patterns on page 16 to trace a total of four top row coffee cups, six middle row coffee cups, and four bottom row coffee cups on paper side of fusible web. Use appropriate fabrics to prepare all appliqués for fusing.

2. Refer to photo on page 13 and layout above to position and fuse appliqués to quilt. Finish appliqué edges with machine satin stitch or other decorative stitching as desired.

Layering and Finishing

1. Referring to Layering the Quilt on page 126. Trim batting to 29" x 27". Arrange and baste backing, batting, and top together. Hand or machine quilt as desired.

2. Refer to Binding the Quilt on page 126. Use 2¾"-wide binding strips to bind quilt.

Bottom Row Coffee Cups

Make 3 (handle separate)
Make 1 (handle & cup traced
as one piece)

Top Row Coffee Cups

Make 2 (handle separate)
Make 2 (handle & cup traced
as one piece)

Cups in the Cupboard Wallhanging

Patterns are reversed for use
with Quick-Fuse Appliqué (page 125)

Tracing Line   —————————
Tracing Line   --------------------
(will be hidden behind other fabrics)

Middle Row Coffee Cups

Make 1 (handle separate)
Make 5 (handle & cup traced
as one piece)

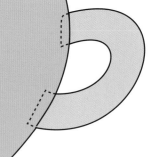

Triple Dash
Tablerunner

1 DAY

Weekend Planner

The simple and nearly neutral color scheme for this runner makes it very versatile. I added 1" accent strips of turquoise to my browns for a touch of visual energy. However, you can keep it completely neutral if you decide to skip adding color.

SATURDAY MORNING

Take a good look at your dining table and room setting to determine your color story. Also confirm that the runner dimensions will work for the size of your table. Make your shopping list and fill your to-go cup with coffee before you hit the fabric store. While shopping, consider if you want to make coordinating napkins. If so, you may want to pick up fabric for those at the same time.

SATURDAY AFTERNOON

Cutting your strips should be about a 30-minute process. Spend a couple more hours putting it all together. Even if you don't usually do your own machine quilting, this project is small enough that you might want to try your hand at it. A walking foot is highly recommended because it will feed your layers (top, batting, backing) evenly and prevent the layers from slipping. To do the quilting and binding, give yourself an additional couple of hours.

How long it will take you to accomplish tasks is an estimate and may vary greatly per individual. You may want to allow extra time for any distractions that may come up – like hunting down your seam ripper. (Happens to the best of us!)

Triple Dash Tablerunner Finished Size: 51" x 16"	FIRST CUT		SECOND CUT	
	Number of Strips or Pieces	Dimensions	Number of Pieces	Dimensions
Fabric A Background ⅝ yard	2 6 3	2½" x 42" 1½" x 42" 1¼" x 42"	7 4 6 12 4	2½" x 6½" 1½" x 20" 1¼" x 15" 1¼" x 2" 1⅛" x 2"
Fabric B Triple Dash ⅙ yard each of 3 Fabrics	2*	2" x 42" *cut for each fabric	3*	2" x 15"
Fabric C Accent Squares & Strips ⅓ yard	3 3	2" x 42" 1" x 42"	2	1" x 20"
Fabric D Accent Strip ⅙ yard	3	1" x 42"	2	1" x 20"
Binding ⅜ yard	4	2¾" x 42"		
Backing - ⅞ yard Batting - 55" x 20"				

Fabric Requirements and Cutting Instructions

Read all instructions before beginning and use ¼"-wide seam allowances throughout. Read Cutting Strips and Pieces on page 124 prior to cutting fabric.

Getting Started

Accent your table with this companion project using the same simple technique as Triple Dash Throw Quilt (pages 9-12). Block measures 6½" square (unfinished). Refer to Accurate Seam Allowance on page 124. Whenever possible use Assembly Line Method on page 124. Press seams in direction of arrows.

Making the Tablerunner

1. Arrange and sew together lengthwise three matching 2" x 15" Fabric B strips and two 1¼" x 15" Fabric A strips as shown to make a strip set. Press. Make three, one of each combination.

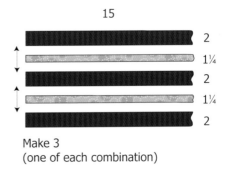

15

2
1¼
2
1¼
2

Make 3 (one of each combination)

2. Cut each strip set from step 1 into two 6½" segments as shown. Cut a total of six segments, two from each strip set.

6½

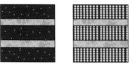

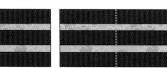

Cut 6 segments
(two of each combination)

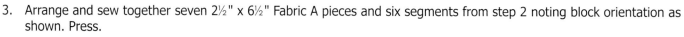

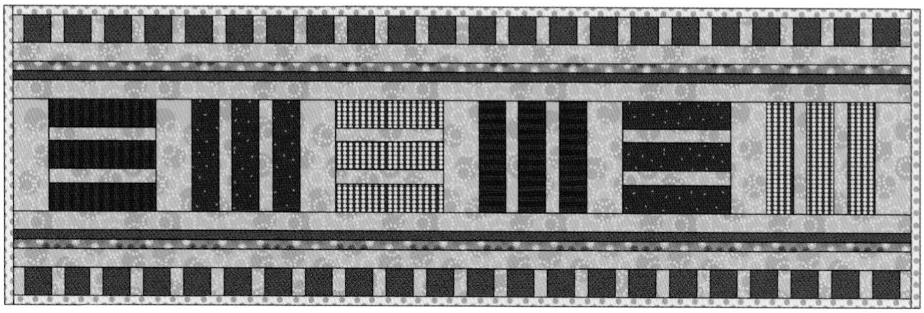

Triple Dash Tablerunner
51" x 16"

3. Arrange and sew together seven 2½" x 6½" Fabric A pieces and six segments from step 2 noting block orientation as shown. Press.

2½   2½   2½   2½   2½   2½   2½

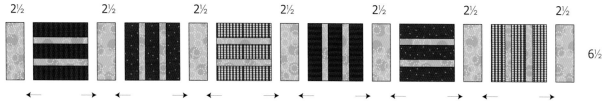

6½

4. Arrange and sew together lengthwise three 2" x 42" Fabric C strips and two 1¼" x 42" Fabric A strips as shown to make a strip set. Press. Cut strip set into fifteen 2"-segments.

2

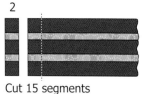

Cut 15 segments

5. Take one segment from step 4 and remove one Fabric C square. Unstitch remaining piece into two segments (includes one Fabric C and one Fabric A piece). Arrange and sew together, two 1⅛" X 2" Fabric A pieces, seven units from step 4, six 1¼" x 2" Fabric A pieces and one unit from this step as shown. Press. Make two.

1⅛   1¼   1¼   1¼   1¼   1¼   1¼   1⅛

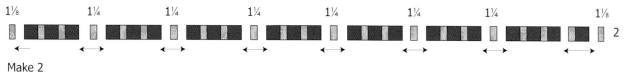

2

Make 2

6. Sew one 1½" x 42" and one 1½" x 20" Fabric A strip end-to-end. Press. Make four. Repeat to sew 1" x 42" and 1" x 20" Fabric C strips end-to-end. Press. Make two. Sew 1" x 42" and 1" x 20" Fabric D strips end-to-end. Press. Make two.

7. Referring to photo on page 17 and layout above and using strips from step 6, sew one 1"-wide Fabric C strip and one 1"-wide Fabric D strip together lengthwise. Press. Make two. Sew one of these units between two 1½"-wide Fabric A strips. Press seams toward Fabric A. Make two.

8. Referring to layout above, arrange and sew together two units from step 5, two units from step 7, and unit from step 3. Press.

Layering and Finishing

1. Cut backing lengthwise into two equal pieces. Sew pieces together to make one 20" x 62" (approximate) backing piece. Press and trim to 20" x 55".

2. Referring to Layering the Quilt on page 126, arrange and baste backing, batting, and top together. Hand or machine quilt as desired.

3. Refer to Binding the Quilt on page 126. Sew 2¾" x 42" binding strips end-to-end to make one continuous 2¾"-wide binding strip. Bind quilt to finish.

1
DAY

Weekend Planner

SATURDAY MORNING

If you've been collecting fabrics for several years you may have an ample personal supply for the block center fabrics. You'll need twenty-one 4½" squares. You may even be able to find a pre-cut set of fabrics that you could trim down to size. Choose a neutral background that will showcase all your lantern colors. Plan to get started on cutting your pieces by mid-morning. You should easily be done with your cutting before lunch. I hope someone is preparing you a grilled cheese sandwich right now.

SATURDAY AFTERNOON

Put your mind to it and you can complete this quilt top in one day. Because this block design is so simple, the piecing will be lickity-split. If the stars are all in alignment today – you may be able to knock it out in no time. Arranging the order of your blocks will take a little playing and a little time. When you are happy, piecing the three rows of blocks should take about 45 minutes. Stitching the border strips will probably take an additional hour. Finish up in another 30 minutes when you add your border strips to the rows of blocks. Oh my gosh, at the rate you're going – you will have time to be taken out to dinner tonight. It is Saturday night after all!

How long it will take you to accomplish tasks is an estimate and may vary greatly per individual. You may want to allow extra time for any distractions that may come up – like hunting down your seam ripper. *(Happens to the best of us!)*

Chinese Lanterns Wallhanging Finished Size: 20" x 31"	FIRST CUT		SECOND CUT	
	Number of Strips or Pieces	Dimensions	Number of Pieces	Dimensions
Fabric A Background ¼ yard	4	1½" x 42"	84	1½" squares
Fabric B Lanterns scrap each of 21 Fabrics	1*	4½" square *cut for each fabric		
Fabric C Row Accent ¼ yard	6	1" x 42"	6	1" x 28½"
Fabric D Row Accent ⅙ yard	4	1" x 42"	4	1" x 28½"
Fabric E Row Accent ⅙ yard	4	1" x 42"	4	1" x 28½"
Fabric F Top & Bottom Border ⅛ yard	1	1½" x 42"	2	1½" x 19½"
Binding ⅓ yard	3	2¾" x 42"		
Backing - ⅔ yard Batting - 24" x 35"				

Fabric Requirements and Cutting Instructions

Read all instructions before beginning and use ¼"-wide seam allowances throughout. Read Cutting Strips and Pieces on page 124 prior to cutting fabric.

Getting Started

For anyone with a stash of fabric, here's the perfect quilt for you! It consists of twenty-one different small pieces of fabric. Block measures 4½" square (unfinished). Refer to Accurate Seam Allowance on page 124. Whenever possible use Assembly Line Method on page 124. Press seams in direction of arrows.

Assembling the Quilt

1. Sew one 1" x 28½" Fabric D strip between one 1" x 28½" Fabric C strip and one 1" x 28½" Fabric E strip as shown. Press. Make four.

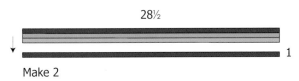

28½

1
1
1

Make 4

2. Sew one 1" x 28½" Fabric C strip to one unit from step 1 as shown. Press. Make two.

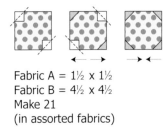

28½

1

Make 2

3. Refer to Quick Corner Triangles on page 124. Making quick corner triangle units, sew two 1½" Fabric A squares to one 4½" Fabric B square as shown. Press. Sew two 1½" Fabric A squares to unit. Press (Note: pressing arrows are in opposite directions). Make twenty-one in assorted fabrics.

Fabric A = 1½ x 1½
Fabric B = 4½ x 4½
Make 21
(in assorted fabrics)

4. Referring to photo on page 20 and layout, arrange blocks from step 3 into three vertical rows with seven blocks each. Sew seven blocks together as shown. Press. Make three.

Make 3

5. Arrange and sew together, two rows from step 1, three rows from step 4, and two rows from step 2 as shown. Press.

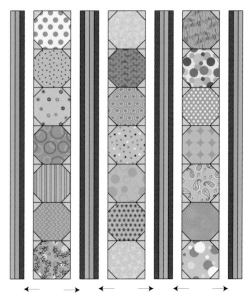

6. Sew 1½" x 19½" Fabric F to top and bottom of quilt. Press seams toward Fabric F.

Layering and Finishing

1. Referring to Layering the Quilt on page 126, arrange and baste backing, batting, and top together. Hand or machine quilt as desired.

2. Refer to Binding the Quilt on page 126. Use 2¾"-wide binding strips to bind quilt.

Chinese Lanterns
Wallhanging 20" x 31"

Modern Four Petal
Flower Quilt

2 DAYS

Weekend Planner

There are usually a few quilts in each of my books that I end up falling in love with. This is one of them! The clean, graphic design, using warm and cool neutrals together, along with a very soothing color story, all contributed to putting it at the top of my favorite list. All that, and it's easy to make too!

FRIDAY EVENING

So that you don't need to leave the house tomorrow morning, shop for your fabrics before you settle in at home for the evening. Don't forget to bring your book with the photo reference and fabric requirements

SATURDAY MORNING

This might be one of those days that you stay in your jammies and slippers 'til noon. But that won't prevent you from getting started on your new project for the weekend. Before you get dressed, make it your goal to cut the pieces and prepare your appliqué shapes. These two tasks will take approximately 2-3 hours. Optional: Take a break to shower and dress.

SATURDAY AFTERNOON

After fusing the appliqué shapes to the blocks, allow another 3 hours to zigzag appliqué the flower shapes.

SUNDAY MORNING

If you skipped the shower entirely yesterday, today is not optional! LOL! Start the quilting part of your day (about 1½ hours) by piecing your blocks.

SUNDAY AFTERNOON

The sashing with the cornerstones deliver a real pop of life to your quilt. It will take a couple of hours to piece your top together. You're awesome — you did it!

How long it will take you to accomplish tasks is an estimate and may vary greatly per individual. You may want to allow extra time for any distractions that may come up - like hunting down your seam ripper. (Happens to the best of us!)

Modern Four Petal Flower Quilt Finished Size: 44½" x 54½"	FIRST CUT		SECOND CUT	
	Number of Strips or Pieces	Dimensions	Number of Pieces	Dimensions
Fabric A Four Petal Flower Block ⅞ yard	3	9½" x 42"	10	9½" squares
Fabric B Cube Block Center ⅛ yard	1	2" x 42"	10	2" squares
Fabric C Cube ⅝ yard	5	3¼" x 42"	20 20	3¼" x 7½" 3¼" x 2"
Fabric D Cube Block Border ½ yard	9	1½" x 42"	20 20	1½" x 9½" 1½" x 7½"
Fabric E Sashing Squares ⅙ yard	2	1½" x 42"	30	1½" squares
Fabric F Sashing ⅔ yard	13	1½" x 42"	49	1½" x 9½"
First Border ¼ yard	5	1" x 42"		
Outside Border ¼ yard	5	1¼" x 42"		
Binding ⅝ yard	5	2¾" x 42"		

Flower Petal Appliqué - ¾ yard
Flower Center Appliqué - scraps
Backing - 2⅞ yards
Batting - 51" x 61"
Lightweight Fusible Web (18"-wide) - 1¾ yards
Stabilizer (20"-wide) - 1½ yards

Fabric Requirements and Cutting Instructions
Read all instructions before beginning and use ¼"-wide seam allowances throughout. Read Cutting Strips and Pieces on page 124 prior to cutting fabric.

Getting Started
This fresh, fashionable quilt with its crisp flowers will add style to a family room. Block measures 9½" square (unfinished). Refer to Accurate Seam Allowance on page 124. Whenever possible use Assembly Line Method on page 124. Press seams in direction of arrows.

Making the Four Petal Flower Block

Refer to appliqué instructions on page 125. Our instructions are for Quick-Fuse Appliqué, but if you prefer hand appliqué, add ¼"-wide seam allowances.

1. Use patterns on page 26 to trace forty leaves and ten circles on paper side of fusible web. Use appropriate fabrics to prepare all appliqués for fusing.

2. Refer to photo on page 23 and diagram below to position and fuse appliqués to 9½" Fabric A squares. Finish appliqué edges with machine satin stitch or other decorative stitching as desired. Make ten. Block measures 9½" square.

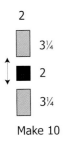

Make 10
Block measures 9½" square

Making the Cube Block

1. Sew one 2" Fabric B square between two 3¼" x 2" Fabric C pieces as shown. Press. Make ten.

2
3¼
2
3¼

Make 10

2. Sew one unit from step 1 between two 3¼" x 7½" Fabric C pieces as shown. Press. Make ten.

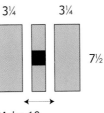

3¼   3¼

7½

Make 10

3. Sew one unit from step 2 between two 1½" x 7½" Fabric D pieces. Press seam toward Fabric D. Sew this unit between two 1½" x 9½" Fabric D pieces as shown. Press. Make ten. Block measures 9½" square.

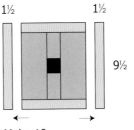

1½   1½

9½

Make 10
Block measures 9½" square

Assembling the Quilt

1. Arrange and sew together five 1½" Fabric E squares and four 1½" x 9½" Fabric F pieces as shown. Press. Make six.

1½   9½   1½   9½   1½   9½   1½   9½   1½

1½

Make 6

2. Arrange and sew together five 1½" x 9½" Fabric F pieces, two Four Petal Flower Blocks and two Cube Blocks as shown. Press. Make five.

1½   1½   1½   1½   1½

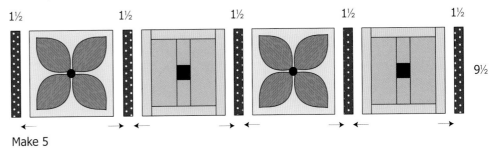

9½

Make 5

3. Referring to layout on page 26, arrange rows from steps 1 and 2 together, alternating the orientation of the block rows. Sew rows together. Press.

Adding the Borders

1. Refer to Adding the Borders on page 126. Sew 1" x 42" First Border strips together end-to-end to make one continuous 1"-wide First Border strip. Measure quilt through center from side to side. Cut two 1"-wide First Border strips to this measurement. Sew to top and bottom of quilt. Press seams toward border.

2. Measure quilt through center from top to bottom including borders just added. Cut two 1"-wide First Border strips to this measurement. Sew to sides of quilt. Press.

3. Refer to steps 1 and 2 to join, measure, trim, and sew 1¼" Outside Border strips to top, bottom, and sides of quilt. Press.

Layering and Finishing

1. Cut backing crosswise into two equal pieces. Sew pieces together lengthwise to make one 51" x 80" (approximate) backing piece. Press and trim to 51" x 61".

2. Referring to Layering the Quilt on page 126, arrange and baste backing, batting, and top together. Hand or machine quilt as desired.

3. Refer to Binding the Quilt on page 126. Sew 2¾" x 42" binding strips end-to-end to make one continuous 2¾"-wide binding strip. Bind quilt to finish.

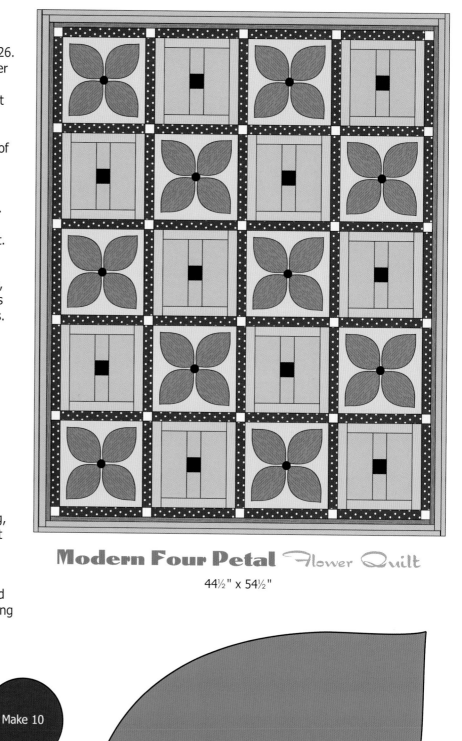

Modern Four Petal Flower Quilt

44½" x 54½"

Make 10

Modern Four Petal Flower Quilt

Make 40

Botanical Burlap
Wall Art

1 DAY

This project is surprisingly easy and using burlap gives a very textured and unique look for wall art. Of course, you can substitute cotton or decorator weight fabric. Customize to your heart's content!

TWO WEEKS PRIOR

Check your art supply store to purchase stretcher bars. If they don't have the sizes you need, you may be able to order from them or try the internet for an online source.

FRIDAY EVENING

Borrow an electric staple gun if you don't have one and put your stretcher bars together tonight. Refer to step 1 on page 29. Make sure it is squared up before stapling. This step only takes about a half hour, but it's nice to have it out of the way.

SATURDAY MORNING

No need to set your alarm too early this morning – you can easily complete this project in one day. Head out to the fabric store to pick up your materials. For more visual texture, I used a variety of fabrics for the leaves, including linen and wool.

SATURDAY AFTERNOON

Fuse interfacing to the back of the large burlap piece to add stability to this loosely woven fabric. Allow an hour to wrap, stretch and staple the background burlap around the stretcher bars. You want it tightly wrapped, however, be careful not to over stretch so the fabric doesn't warp and look misshapen.

You can quickly cut out your leaf appliqués in about 30 minutes. Fusing, appliquéing and top-stitching the veins on the leaves will take the most time for this project – probably a couple of hours. Allow another 45 minutes to fray and fuse the leaf blocks to the background. Voila- you're done! No quilting necessary to finish this project.

How long it will take you to accomplish tasks is an estimate and may vary greatly per individual. You may want to allow extra time for any distractions that may come up – like hunting down your seam ripper. (Happens to the best of us!)

Getting Started
This 26" x 38" wall art has a twist; it is made using burlap fabric as are its companion projects. Appliqués are made from assorted wool and cotton fabrics adding texture and pattern to wall art. Interfacing was placed on the wrong side of burlap to add stability. Read all instructions before beginning.

Supplies

Fabric A - Background - 1 yard (Burlap)
  One 31" x 42" piece
Fabric B - Appliqué Background (Burlap)
(cut for each of two fabrics) - ⅜ yard
  Three 11" squares
Appliqués - Assorted scraps
  (linen, wool & cotton)
Iron-on Lightweight Interfacing - 3 yards
Lightweight Fusible Web (18"-wide) - 2 yards
Stablilizer (20"-wide) - 2 yards
Two 38" and two 26" Stretcher Bars
Staple Gun & Staples
Picture or Sawtooth Hanger

Making the Wall Art
Refer to appliqué instructions on page 125. Our instructions are for Quick-Fuse Appliqué, but if you prefer hand appliqué add ¼"-wide seam allowances.

1. Referring to Burlap Preparation, center and fuse one 10" interfacing square to the wrong side of one 11" Fabric B square following manufacturer's instructions. Make six, three of each combination.

2. Using a narrow zigzag stitch, stitch on edge of interfacing. Project will be frayed to stitched edge. Make six, three of each combination.

3. Use pattern on page 29 to trace twenty-four leaves on paper side of fusible web. Use appropriate fabrics to prepare all appliqués for fusing.

4. Refer to photo on page 27 to position and fuse appliqués to units from step 2. Refer to Tip for Marking Veins on page 29. Using removable fabric marker, draw vein lines on each leaf. Finish appliqué edges with machine satin stitch or other decorative stitching as desired. Stitch veins by machine using a straight stitch.

5. Draw six 10" squares on paper-side of fusible web. Cut on traced line. Center and fuse each square to wrong side of units from step 4.

6. Referring to photo on page 27, fray outside edge of blocks to stitching lines.

Burlap Preparation
Lay burlap on a flat surface and align grain lines as straight as possible. Use iron-on interfacing to stabilize burlap following manufacturer's instructions. Follow step-by-step instructions for further treatment.

Finishing the Wall Art

1. Using interlocking stretcher bars, slide two 38" and two 26" bars together. Check for square by measuring diagonally from corner to corner. Staple at corners.

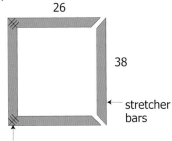

26

38

stretcher bars

staples

2. Prepare 31" x 42" Fabric A piece by adhering iron-on interfacing to wrong side, following instructions on Burlap Preparation on page 28.

3. Center frame on wrong side of Fabric A piece. Pull fabric around frame, staple in the middle on each side pulling fabric tight to obtain good tension. Turn piece over to check alignment. Continue process, working from center, stretching and stapling fabric, stopping at corner.

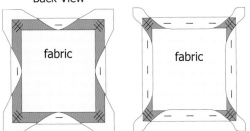

Back View

fabric

fabric

4. Pull corner tight and check from front side to make sure fabric is taut. Cut extra bulk from corners if desired. Fold fabric at 90°, crease, and form corner. Staple tightly to back. Attach a wire picture hanger or sawtooth hanger.

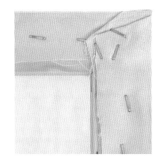

5. Referring to photo on page 27, center and fuse six appliqué squares to background alternating Fabric B placement. Note: For ease in pressing, place a folded towel under center of wall art to add stability.

Burlap Collection

Pattern is reversed for use
with Quick-Fuse Appliqué (page 125)

Tracing Line _____

Embroidery Placement ....

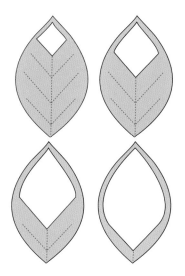

Tip for Marking Veins

Trace four leaf patterns with veins on template plastic, pattern paper or cardstock. Cut out each vein opening as shown above creating four separate patterns. Trace each vein line in succession. After veins are marked draw a centerline as shown in original pattern.

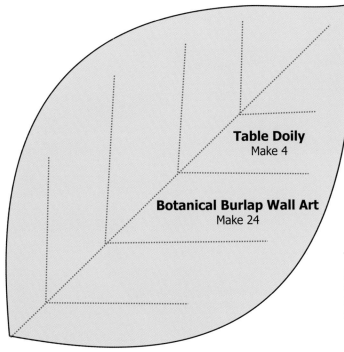

Table Doily
Make 4

Botanical Burlap Wall Art
Make 24

Burlap
Collection

2 DAYS

30

Goodness! I just love this fun, graphic and organic looking table ensemble. Again, using the burlap adds textural visual interest. Sometimes this trendy burlap look isn't always practical to put in your home since it sheds and is scratchy. In small doses, like these projects, it's a perfect way to utilize the material.

SATURDAY MORNING – Combine picking up your fabrics along with other errands this morning. Take the time to stop at the coffee drive-through for a Grande Mocha on your way home. It sets the mood for a fun afternoon. That's all it will take to create this fun pair since the techniques are simple and the scale is small.

SATURDAY AFTERNOON – It will likely take you about an hour each to put together the runner and the doily. Allow an additional 1 to 1½ hours to add the binding to the runner and an extra 15 minutes to fray the doily. Get caught up on your favorite HGTV program while hand stitching the binding. Think about using a fun backing for the table runner to make it reversible!

WINE LOVER GIFT BAG

Make it a mission to save your wine bottle corks for the finishing touch on this project. After you decide on fabrics, it only takes about an hour of sewing to stitch up this unique wine gift bag.

GIFT CARD BAG

I know everyone loves to receive gift cards, but sometimes I feel I want to add a personal touch to my gift. Using up scraps can create a unique gift bag in an hour and a quarter. (Less time than shopping!!)

DECORATIVE TOASTER COVER

A toaster is best known as the quintessential boring wedding gift. Imagine if it was received with its own custom toaster cover! I break out in a big grin every time I look at this — it's so cute! Special projects do take a little time. From start to finish, plan on a good 3½ hours to put this project together.

How long it will take you to accomplish tasks is an estimate and may vary greatly per individual. You may want to allow extra time for any distractions that may come up – like hunting down your seam ripper. (Happens to the best of us!)

Tablerunner and Doily

Fabric Requirements and Cutting Instructions

Read all instructions before beginning and use ¼"-wide seam allowances throughout. Read Cutting Strips and Pieces on page 124 prior to cutting fabric.

Getting Started
Simple designs enhanced with the play of burlap and cotton fabrics in various geometric scales, make this a great contemporary addition to a table.

Making the Table Doily

Refer to appliqué instructions on page 125. Our instructions are for Quick-Fuse Appliqué, but if you prefer hand appliqué add ¼"-wide seam allowances.

1. Cut four 5" x 20" and one 7½" square from interfacing. Referring to manufacturer's instructions, fuse interfacing to wrong side of four 5" x 20" Fabric B pieces and 7½" Fabric A square.

2. Referring to Mitered Borders on page 127, sew four Fabric B units from step 1 to top, bottom, and sides of 7½" Fabric A square, mitering corners. Trim and press seams toward Fabric A.

3. Use pattern on page 29 to trace four leaves on paper side of fusible web. Use appropriate fabrics to prepare all appliqués for fusing.

Table Doily Finished Size: 14" square	FIRST CUT		SECOND CUT	
	Number of Strips or Pieces	Dimensions	Number of Pieces	Dimensions
Fabric A Center Scrap	1	7½" square		
Fabric B Border (Burlap) ⅓ yard	2	5" x 42"	4	5" x 20"
Backing Fat Quarter	1	14" square		
Appliqués - Scraps Lightweight Fusible Web (18"-wide) - ⅝ yard Iron-on Interfacing - ¾ yard Stabilizer (20"-wide) - ½ yard Removable Fabric Marker				

4. Referring to photo on page 30, mark leaf placement on background by tracing around leaf template with removable fabric marker. Since mitered seams are bulky, cut away inside marked leaf area trimming approximately ⅜"-½" inside drawn line.

5. Position and fuse appliqués to unit from step 4 being sure to cover trimmed area.

6. Finish appliqué edges with machine satin stitch or other decorative stitching as desired. Refer to Tip for Marking Veins on page 29, to mark and sew leaf veins. Square unit to 14".

7. Draw and cut a 13" square on paper-side of fusible web. Fuse to wrong side of 14" backing piece. Cut on drawn line.

8. Center and fuse backing piece to wrong side of doily unit from step 6.

9. Using a narrow zigzag stitch, stitch on edge of backing. Fringe outside edge of burlap to stitching line. Note: Remove iron-on interfacing as needed.

Making the Tablerunner

1. Referring to Burlap Preparation on page 28, cut and fuse 10½" x 24½" interfacing to 10½" x 24½" Fabric A piece.

2. Arrange and sew together two 4½" x 10½" Fabric D pieces, two 1½" x 10½" Fabric C pieces, two 1" x 10½" Fabric B piece, and Fabric A piece as shown. Press.

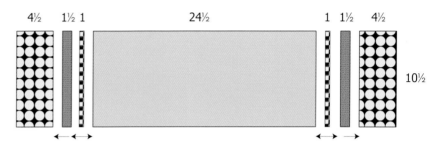

3. Referring to Layering the Quilt on page 126, arrange and baste backing and top wrong sides together. There is no batting used for this project, just stitch in the ditch to hold backing in place.

4. Refer to Making Bias Strips on page 126 and Binding the Quilt on page 126. Use 2¾"-wide binding strips to bind quilt.

5. Referring to photo on page 30, layer doily on tablerunner and tack in place, if desired.

Burlap Tablerunner Finished Size: 36" x 11"	FIRST CUT		SECOND CUT	
	Number of Strips or Pieces	Dimensions	Number of Pieces	Dimensions
Fabric A Background (Burlap) ⅜ yard	1	10½" x 42"	1	10½" x 24½"
Fabric B Accent Trim ⅛ yard	1	1" x 42"	2	1" x 10½"
Fabric C Accent Trim ⅛ yard	1	1½" x 42"	2	1½" x 10½"
Fabric D Outside Border ¼ yard	1	4½" x 42"	2	4½" x 10½"
Bias Binding ⅝ yard for Bias - 2¾" Bias strips cut from 19" square OR ⅓ yard for Straight Cuts (3 strips - 2¾" x 42") Backing - ⅜ yard Iron-on Interfacing - ¾ yard				

Wine Lover Gift Bag

Fabric Requirements and Cutting Instructions

Read all instructions before beginning and use ¼"-wide seam allowances throughout. Read Cutting Strips and Pieces on page 124 prior to cutting fabric.

Getting Started
Select your favorite vintage wine and wrap it up in this easy-to-make wine cover creating a great hostess gift.

Making the Wine Bag

1. To prevent burlap from fraying while constructing bag follow this step. Lay 10" x 14½" Fabric A piece on a flat surface aligning grain lines as straight as possible. Mark 8" x 12½" rectangle in the center of fabric; this will be the cutting line. Using a zigzag stitch, sew just inside the marked line. Cut on marked line. Note: Delete this step if using cotton fabric and cut piece to measure 8" x 12½".

2. Sew 8" x 12½" Fabric A piece between one 1½" x 12½" Fabric B strip and one 2½" x 12½" Fabric D strips as shown. Press.

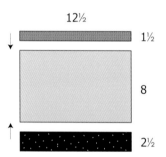

3. Fold unit from step 2 lengthwise, right sides together, to make a 6¼" x 11" folded piece. Using ¼"-wide seam, sew side and bottom (Fabric D) edges leaving top (Fabric B) edge free of stitches. Turn right side out and press.

4. Fold one bottom corner of unit from step 5, matching side seam to bottom seam. Draw a 1½" line ⅞" from bottom corner as shown. Sew on drawn line, anchoring stitches at each end. Repeat for other side.

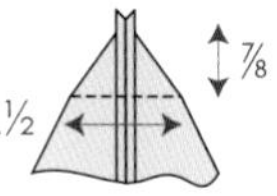

5. Fold stitched corners to bottom seam of bag and tack in place for added stability.

6. Fold 6½" x 12½" Fabric C piece in half crosswise, right sides together, to make a 6½" x 6¼" folded piece. Sew 6½" sides together. Turn right side out and press.

7. Fold tube from step 1 in half lengthwise wrong sides together, to make a 3¼" x 6¼" folded piece. Press. Insert unit from step 5 into this unit matching raw edges. Using ¼"-wide seam, sew along raw edges. Turn right side out and press.

8. For the closure, drill a hole in the center of two corks making hole a little larger than yarn/cording dimension. Thread yarn/cording through one cork. Tie a knot to hold cork in place. Repeat for other end. Place wine in bag and refer to photo on page 30 to tie yarn/cording to close bag.

Wine Lover Gift Bag Finished Size: 6" x 13"	FIRST CUT	
	Number of Strips or Pieces	Dimensions
Fabric A Main Section (Burlap) ⅓ yard	1	10" x 14½"
Fabric B Accent Scrap	1	1½" x 12½"
Fabric C Top Section ¼ yard	1	6½" x 12½"
Fabric D Bottom Section ⅛ yard	1	2½" x 12½"
Yarn or Cording - ⅝ yard Cork - 2 Drill or Awl		

Gift Card Bag

Fabric Requirements and Cutting Instructions
Read all instructions before beginning and use ¼"-wide seam allowances throughout. Read Cutting Strips and Pieces on page 124 prior to cutting fabric.

Getting Started
Place a gift card or small gift for someone special in this charming bag.

Making the Bag

1. To prevent burlap from fraying while constructing bag follow this step. Lay 6" x 14" Fabric A piece on a flat surface aligning grain lines as straight as possible. Mark 4½" x 12½" rectangle in the center of fabric; this will be the cutting line. Using a zigzag stitch, sew just inside the marked line. Cut on marked line. Note: Delete this step if using cotton fabric and cut piece to measure 4½" x 12½".

2. Sew 1" x 12½" Fabric B piece to one 4" x 12½" Fabric C piece as shown. Press.

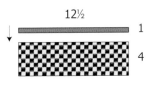

3. Fold unit from step 2 crosswise, right sides together, to make a 6¼" x 4½" folded piece. Using ¼"-wide seam, sew side and bottom (Fabric C) edges leaving top (Fabric B) edge free of stitches. Turn right side out and press.

4. Fold one bottom corner of unit from step 3, matching side seam to bottom seam. Draw a 1½" line ⅞" from bottom corner as shown. Sew on drawn line, anchoring stitches at each end. Repeat for other side.

5. Fold stitched corners to bottom seam of bag and tack in place for added stability.

6. Fold 4½" x 12½" Fabric A piece in half crosswise to make a 4½" x 6¼" folded piece. Sew 4½" sides together. Turn right side out and press.

7. Fold tube from step 6 in half lengthwise wrong sides together, to make a 2¼" x 6¼" folded piece. Press. Insert unit from step 5 into this unit matching raw edges. Using ¼"-wide seam, sew along raw edges. Turn right side out and press.

8. Refer to photo on page 30 for handle placement. Cut two pieces of cording to desired length, one piece will be used on each side. Tie a knot to both cording ends and stitch ends to bag. Repeat for other side.

Gift Card Bag Finished Size: 6" x 8"	FIRST CUT	
	Number of Strips or Pieces	Dimensions
Fabric A — Bag Top (Burlap) ¼ yard	1	6" x 14"
Fabric B — Bag Accent Scrap	1	1" x 12½"
Fabric C — Bag Bottom ⅛ yard	1	4 " x 12½"
Handles (Jute) - ⅝ yard		

Decorative Toaster Cover

Fabric Requirements and Cutting Instructions

Read all instructions before beginning and use ¼"-wide seam allowances throughout. Check the pattern against your toaster and adjust sizes as needed if necessary.

Getting Started

Dress up your toaster with this stylish cover. All sections are quilted prior to sewing sections together then bound on the outside giving the look of piping.

Making the Cover

1. Sew 1¼" x 42" Fabric B strip between 6" x 42" Fabric A strip and 3" x 42" Fabric C strip as shown.

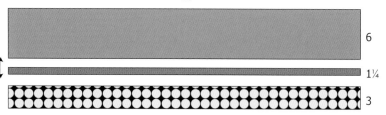

2. Referring to Layering the Quilt on page 126, arrange and baste 13" x 42" lining, batting, and unit from step 1 together. Hand or machine quilt as desired.

3. Using Toaster Cover Pattern on page 36, trace pattern and a reversed image on pattern paper or template plastic aligning placement lines to make a whole pattern. Trace horizontal lines on pattern. Place pattern on unit from step 1 aligning placement lines on accent seam allowance as shown. Trace pattern and cut on traced line. Mark and cut two. These are the cover's front and back pieces.

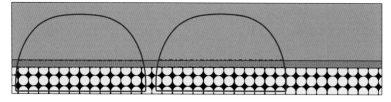

4. Referring to Layering the Quilt on page 126, arrange, baste, and quilt 8" x 30" Fabric C, lining and batting pieces. Trim quilted strip to measure 7" x 28". This is the cover's side unit. Mark center of strip with pins. Measure 13" from center and mark with pins on both sides. These will be guides for sewing pieces together.

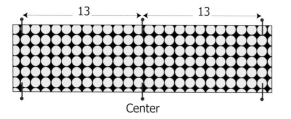

Center

Decorative Toaster Cover Finished Size: 8" x 13" x 6"	FIRST CUT	
	Number of Strips or Pieces	Dimensions
Fabric A Front Top Section (Burlap) ¼ yard	1	6" x 42"
Fabric B Accent ⅛ yard	1	1¼" x 42"
Fabric C Front & Back Bottom Section and Side ⅜ yard	1 1	8" x 30" 3" x 42"
Fabric D Handle Scrap	1	5" x 8½"
Side Binding ¼ yard	2	2¼" x 42"
Bottom Binding ⅙ yard	1	2¾" x 42"
Lining ⅔ yard	1 1	8" x 30" 13" x 42"
Batting	1 1	8" x 30" 13" x 42"

5. Fold 5" x 8½" Fabric D piece in half lengthwise and press. Open and fold raw edges to center pressed line. Press. Fold again in half lengthwise. Press. Top stitch folds in place. This will be the handle for cover.

6. Find center for front, back, and side units and mark with pins. Align handle on side unit center marks matching raw edges. Baste in place.
Note: Units will be sewn with wrong sides (lining pieces) together with seams to the outside. After pieces are sewn they will be covered with binding to give a piping effect. The other marked pins are used for a guide to determine distance from center to bottom edge. They may be off of the cover but still can be used to make sure both sides measure the same distance from center.

7. Pin front to side unit matching center pins, lining sides together, and handle showing on outside edge. Ease top piece along side edge, pinning every ¼". Using ¼" seam allowance, sew pieces together.

8. Pin and sew back piece to unit from step 7 matching pin placements. Trim any excess fabric from side strip as needed.

9. Refer to Binding the Quilt on page 126. Sew 2¼" x 42" binding strips to side seam edges and 2¾" x 42" binding strip for bottom edge.

Toaster Cover Pattern

Tracing Line ————————

Placement Line ––·––·––·––·––·

Trace pattern and placement lines.
Trace reverse image aligning trace line and placement lines to make a whole toaster pattern.
Adjust pattern if necessary to fit toaster.

Decorator Dot
Quilt

2 DAYS

Weekend Planner

THURSDAY EVENING

On your way home from work; treat yourself to a mid-week trip to your quilt shop to pick out fabrics. I have a cream colored leathered sofa which was my inspiration for choosing my color scheme. But take this any direction you want. Since you only need 6" squares for the dots, you may be able to gather several of these from your scrap shelf. The fabric that I used in the border is a printed dot pattern. Choose six ivories, six blacks and your border fabrics tonight.

FRIDAY EVENING

Take care of these two simple tasks tonight and you'll thank yourself in the morning. Prepare your circle template by tracing the 5" circle onto a clear piece of plastic or cardboard. Cut out the circle and it's ready to use. Also, set the timer on your coffee maker, so you'll wake up to the aroma of fresh coffee in the morning. Great inspiration for an early start in the morning!

SATURDAY MORNING

Tracing your circles, fusing and cutting out the big dots will likely take about an hour and a half. The block squares and border strips will be fast to cut out — about 45 minutes should cover it. Allow some time to appliqué the circles to the background squares. (Less than 2 hours) Remember to use tear-away stabilizer behind the appliqués. It should take about 20 minutes to tear away the stabilizer after your appliqués are complete. This has been a very full and productive morning. Take the rest of the day for other weekend activities

SUNDAY AFTERNOON

After having brunch with the family, ask them to do the dishes since you plan to spend the rest of the afternoon finishing up the quilt top. Arrange your blocks in a visually pleasing way. Organize your blocks on your design wall or floor so you can keep track of the arrangement. Some people like to track this by numbering their blocks with a little piece of masking tape. BE SURE not to iron over the tape, because it will leave a nasty sticky residue if you do. A couple hours later you should be finished with your top.

How long it will take you to accomplish tasks is an estimate and may vary greatly per individual. You may want to allow extra time for any distractions that may come up – like hunting down your seam ripper. (Happens to the best of us!)

Decorator Dot Quilt Finished Size: 37½" x 50½"	FIRST CUT		SECOND CUT	
	Number of Strips or Pieces	Dimensions	Number of Pieces	Dimensions
Fabric A Background ½ yard each of 6 Fabrics	2*	7" x 42" *cut for each fabric	6*	7" squares
Fabric B Circles/Dots ¼ yard each of 6 Fabrics	1*	6" x 42" *cut for each fabric	6*	5" Circles (see step 1)
First Border ¼ yard	5	1" x 42"	2	1" x 33"
Second Border ¼ yard	5	1" x 42"	2	1" x 34"
Outside Border ⅓ yard	5	1½" x 42"	2	1½" x 35"
Binding ½ yard	5	2¾" x 42"		

Backing - 2½ yards
Batting - 44" x 57"
Lightweight Fusible Web (18"-wide) - 2 yards
Template Plastic
Stabilizer (20"-wide) - 2 yards

Fabric Requirements and Cutting Instructions
Read all instructions before beginning and use ¼"-wide seam allowances throughout. Read Cutting Strips and Pieces on page 124 prior to cutting fabric.

Getting Started
An elegant contemporary quilt, with its combination of various shades of lights and darks, makes a striking statement. Block measures 7" square (unfinished). Refer to Accurate Seam Allowance on page 124. Whenever possible use Assembly Line Method on page 124. Press seams in direction of arrows.

Adding the Appliqués
Refer to appliqué instructions on page 125. Our instructions are for Quick-Fuse Appliqué, but if you prefer hand appliqué add ¼"-wide seam allowances.

1. Use pattern on page 127 to make 5" circle template. Using template, trace thirty-five circles on paper side of fusible web. Cut ¼" from both sides of drawn circle line as shown. This will remove the center section of fusible web to help reduce bulk and stiffness. Use Fabric B strips to prepare all appliqués for fusing.

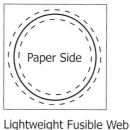

Paper Side

Lightweight Fusible Web
Trace Line ————————
Cut Line – – – – – –

2. Center and fuse appliqués to assorted 7" Fabric A squares. Finish appliqué edges with machine satin stitch or other decorative stitching as desired. This quilt used a zigzag stitch on circles. Additional time is needed for satin stitching. Optional: From the wrong side of block cut away the center background area of each circle being careful not to cut Fabric B.

Assembling and Adding the Borders

1. Refer to photo on page 37 and layout to arrange all blocks into seven rows with five blocks each. There will be one block remaining.

2. Sew five blocks together as shown. Press. Make seven rows pressing seams in opposite direction from row to row.

Make 7
(in assorted combinations)

3. Sew rows together and press.

4. Refer to Adding the Borders on page 126. Sew two 1" x 33" First Border strips to top and bottom of quilt. Press seams toward border.

5. Sew two 1" x 42" First Border strips together end-to-end to make one continuous 1"-wide First Border strip. Measure quilt through center from top to bottom including borders just added. Cut two 1"-wide First Border strips to this measurement. Sew to sides of quilt. Press.

6. Sew two 1" x 34" Second Border strips to top and bottom of quilt. Press seams toward border just sewn. Refer to step 5 to join, measure, trim, and sew 1"-wide Second Border strips to sides of quilt. Press.

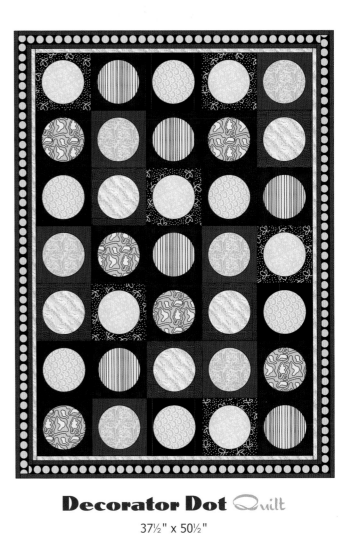

Decorator Dot Quilt

37½" x 50½"

7. Sew two 1½" x 35" Outside Border strips to top and bottom of quilt. Press seams toward border just sewn. Refer to step 5 to join, measure, trim, and sew 1½"-wide Outside Border strips to sides of quilt. Press.

Layering and Finishing

1. Cut backing crosswise into two equal pieces. Sew pieces together lengthwise to make one 45" x 80" (approximate) backing piece. Press and trim to 45" x 58".

2. Referring to Layering the Quilt on page 126, arrange and baste backing, batting, and top together. Hand or machine quilt as desired.

3. Refer to Binding the Quilt on page 126. Sew 2¾" x 42" binding strips end-to-end to make one continuous 2¾"-wide binding strip. Bind quilt to finish.

Fashion Bed
Queen Quilt

1 DAY

Weekend Planner

Even though this is a large full-sized bed quilt, it may be the quickest and easiest quilt to complete in the entire book thanks to large simple blocks. This is the type of quilt design that you see at retail and can cost a bundle. Make it yourself and use custom colors chosen just for your room.

SATURDAY MORNING

After a big bowl of Wheaties, hit the quilt shop with lots of energy. It's going to be a fun day of shopping and sewing! If you like the look of this bed quilt, look for patterns that have similar visual "weight" — in other words, don't make some too dark and some too light. Because of the large scale of the blocks, look for medium to large scale prints also. When you find complementary colors that you love, also choose a variety of types of patterns (i.e. floral, paisley, dot, stripe, tonal, etc.), as well as some variety in the scale. Keeping all that in mind, select 8 fabrics that you like together. Sometimes you can find an assortment of patterns from the same collection that may work together very well. The sewing will be fast, so you can spend the whole morning making your choices.

SATURDAY AFTERNOON

Clear off the entire dining room table to make room to cut your fabrics. Allow yourself an hour for cutting. Piece all the stripe blocks first and then the four-patch blocks. You should be able to knock that out in the next hour. Gosh, in another hour you can piece together the entire top. Press the top very well before you send it to your favorite machine quilter.

How long it will take you to accomplish tasks is an estimate and may vary greatly per individual. You may want to allow extra time for any distractions that may come up – like hunting down your seam ripper. (Happens to the best of us!)

Fashion Bed Queen Quilt Finished Size: 91" x 97"	FIRST CUT		SECOND CUT	
	Number of Strips or Pieces	Dimensions	Number of Pieces	Dimensions
Fabric A 1¼ yards each of 4 Fabrics	5*	8" x 42" *cut for each fabric	5*	8" x 32½"
Fabric B 1 yard each of 4 Fabrics	2*	15½" x 42" *cut for each fabric	4*	15½" x 16½"
Binding 1 yard	10	2¾" x 42"		
Backing - 8¼ yards Batting - 99" x 105"				

Fabric Requirements and Cutting Instructions
Read all instructions before beginning and use ¼"-wide seam allowances throughout. Read Cutting Strips and Pieces on page 124 prior to cutting fabric.

Getting Started
Let your fabrics make the fashion statement in this quick-to-make queen-size quilt. Block measures 30½" x 32½" (unfinished). Refer to Accurate Seam Allowance on page 124. Whenever possible use Assembly Line Method on page 124. Press seams in direction of arrows.

Making the Quilt

1. Arrange and sew together four 8" x 32½" Fabric A pieces, one of each variation. Press. Make five and label Unit 1.

Unit 1

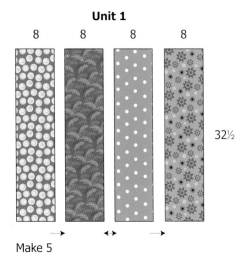

Make 5

2. Sew two different 15½" x 16½" Fabric B pieces together in pairs. Press. Make four matching units. Repeat to sew remaining fabrics together in pairs. Press. Make four.

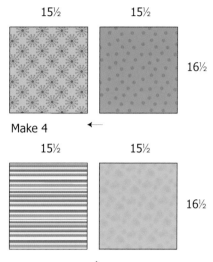

15½   15½

16½

Make 4   ←

15½   15½

16½

Make 4   →

3. Sew two different units from step 2 together as shown. Refer to Twisting Seams on page 124. Press. Make four and label Unit 2.

Unit 2

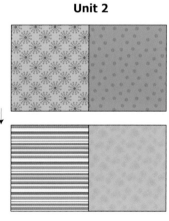

Make 4

Assembling and Finishing the Quilt

1. Referring to layout below, arrange and sew together two of Unit 1 and one of Unit 2. Press seams toward Unit 1. Make two.

2. Referring to layout below, arrange and sew together two of Unit 2 and one Unit 1. Press seams toward Unit 1.

3. Referring to layout below, sew row from step 2 between two rows from step 1. Press.

4. Cut backing crosswise into three equal pieces. Sew pieces together lengthwise to make one 99" x 120" (approximate) backing piece. Press and trim to 99" x 105".

5. Referring to Layering the Quilt on page 126, arrange and baste backing, batting, and top together. Hand or machine quilt as desired.

6. Refer to Binding the Quilt on page 126. Sew 2¾" x 42" binding strips end-to-end to make one continuous 2¾"-wide binding strip. Bind quilt to finish.

Fashion Bed Queen Quilt
91" x 97"

Fashion
Decorative Pillows

Fabric Requirements and Cutting
Instructions
Read all instructions before beginning and use ¼"-wide seam allowances throughout. Read Cutting Strips and Pieces on page 124 prior to cutting fabric.

Getting Started
Here are two different pillow styles to adorn your bed; Pillow #1 finishes at 12" and Pillow #2 finishes at 15". Press seams in direction of arrows.

Making Pillow #1

1. Draw a triangle on pattern paper or template plastic as shown with two short sides measuring 7" and angle side measuring a little less than 10". Cut out triangle on traced line.

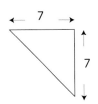

2. Use triangle pattern from step 1 to cut four triangles each from Fabric A and Fabric B.

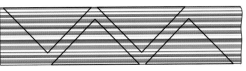

Cut for directional fabric.

3. Sew one Fabric A triangle to one Fabric B triangle as shown. Press. Make four. Square to 6½". Press two as shown (use in step 4). Press two in the opposite direction (use in step 5).

Make 4
(Press two in opposite direction for step 5)
Square to 6½"

4. Refer to Quick Corner Triangles on page 124. Making a quick corner triangle unit, sew one 3½" Fabric C square to one unit from step 3 as shown. Press. Make two.

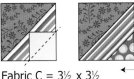

Fabric C = 3½ x 3½
Unit from step 3
Make 2

Decorative Pillow 1 Finished Size: 12" x 12"	FIRST CUT	
	Number of Strips or Pieces	Dimensions
Fabric A Background ¼ yard	4	7" triangles (see steps 1 & 2)
Fabric B Accent Border ¼ yard	4	7" triangles (see steps 1 & 2)
Fabric C Center Scrap	2	3½" squares
Fabric D Center Scrap	2	3½" squares
Backing ⅓ yard	2	9" x 12½"
Batting & Lining - 16" square each (Lining doesn't show) Pillow Form - 12" Pillow Form		

5. Making a quick corner triangle unit, sew one 3½" Fabric D square to one unit from step 3 as shown. Press. Make two.

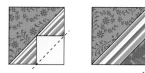

Fabric D = 3½ x 3½
Unit from step 3
Make 2

6. Sew one unit from step 4 to one unit from step 5 as shown. Press. Make two. Press. Sew units together. Refer to Twisting Seams on page 124. Press. Go to Finishing the Pillows to complete project.

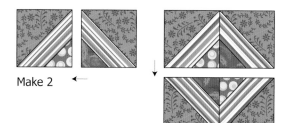

Make 2

Making Pillow #2

1. Sew two 4" Fabric A squares, one of each variation, as shown. Press. Make two. Sew units together, as shown. Refer to Twisting Seams on page 124. Press.

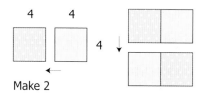

4   4   4

Make 2

2. Sew unit from step 1 between two 1" x 7½" Fabric B pieces. Press seams toward Fabric B. Sew this unit between two 1" x 8½" Fabric B pieces. Press.

3. Sew unit from step 2 between two 1" x 8½" Fabric C pieces. Press seams toward Fabric C. Sew this unit between two 1" x 9½" Fabric C pieces. Press.

4. Referring to Mitered Borders on page 127, sew 3½" x 20" Fabric D strips to top, bottom, and sides of quilt, mitering corners. Press seams toward Fabric D.

Fashion Decorative Pillow #1
12" x 12"

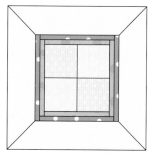

Fashion Decorative Pillow #2
15" x 15"

Finishing the Pillows

1. Refer to Finishing Pillows on page 127, step 1, to prepare pillow top for quilting. Quilt as desired.

2. For Pillow #1 prepare two 9" x 12½" backing pieces and refer to Finishing Pillows, page 127, steps 2-4, to sew backing.

3. For Pillow #2, prepare two 10½" x 15½" backing pieces and refer to Finishing Pillows, page 127, steps 2-4, to sew backing.

4. Insert 12" pillow form for Pillow #1, 15" pillow form for Pillow #2 or refer to Pillow Forms page 127 to make a pillow form if desired.

Decorative Pillow 2 Finished Size: 15" x 15"	FIRST CUT	
	Number of Strips or Pieces	Dimensions
Fabric A Center Scraps each of 2 Fabrics	2*	4" squares *cut for each fabric
Fabric B Accent Border ⅛ yard	2 2	1" x 8½" 1" x 7½"
Fabric C Accent Border ⅛ yard	2 2	1" x 9½" 1" x 8½"
Fabric D Outside Border ¼ yard	4	3½" x 20"
Backing ⅜ yard	2	10½" x 15½"
Batting & Lining - 19" square each (Lining doesn't show) Pillow Form - 15" Pillow Form		

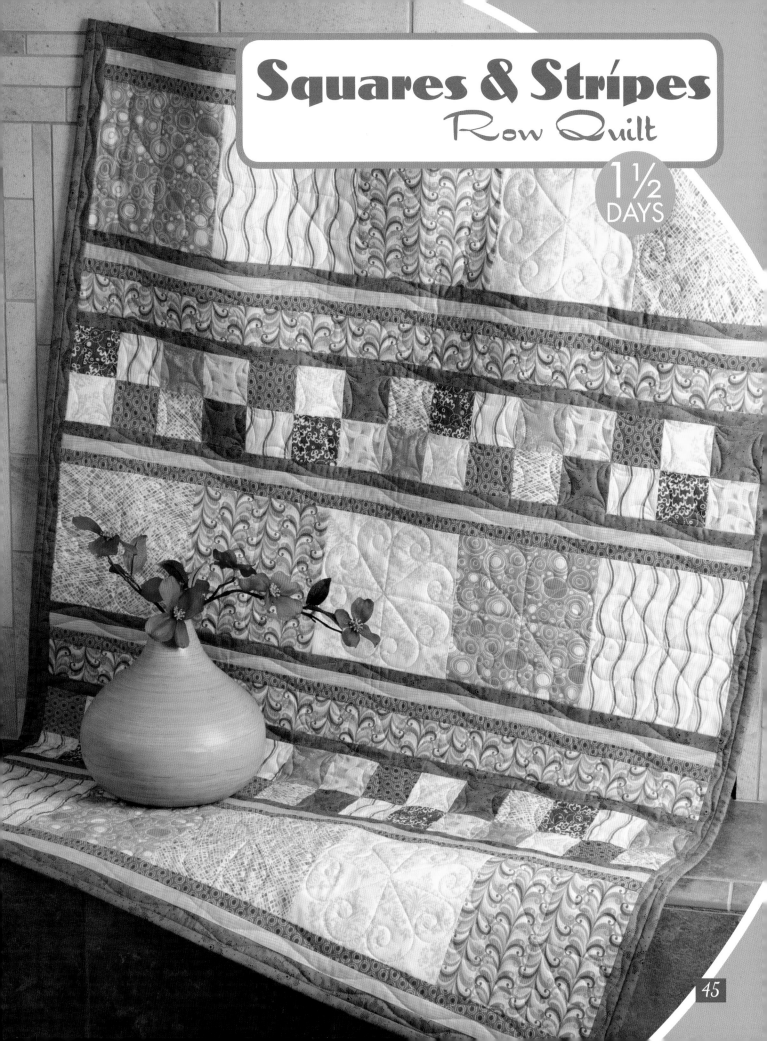

Squares & Stripes
Row Quilt

1½ DAYS

Weekend Planner

Since this quilt design is so simple, this is a fun one to use some wilder patterned fabrics. I really had a blast putting this assortment of ultra-modern colors together. It's so refreshing to work outside your typical comfort zone. (A little secret...I kind of enjoy the reaction I get by shocking people when I make unexpected fabric choices!)

SATURDAY MORNING

Oh, shopping for fabrics – what a fabulous way to spend your morning! Amongst these wild prints, be sure to include some quieter, calmer prints too. You need some breathing room. That is particularly important for the 1¼" strips. Also, if you choose prints that have varied visual effect and different scale, they will look more interesting when pieced next to each other

SATURDAY AFTERNOON

Cutting the strips and pieces for this one will be a snap since there are only two sizes of squares and two sizes of strips. I bet in an hour and a half you have it all cut and ready to go. Since this design isn't too complicated to piece, I would put a movie on in the background to keep you company. Maybe the movie "Speed" will inspire you to, well... "speed" through your piecing. Tackle the rows of squares first and then the stripped border sets. If the movie was appropriately inspiring, you'll have this knocked out in about 3 hours. Call it a day and finish up tomorrow after you've had an evening of rest.

SUNDAY AFTERNOON

Weekend mornings fly by no matter what. If you're anything like me – I like to take a weekend morning to sleep in and start my day slow over a hunky-sized mug of coffee. By the time I'm showered and ready to go, it's noon! I'm really relaxed because I know this top can be pieced together in less than a couple hours. There is even time left to clean up your sewing area this afternoon to make way for the next project...

How long it will take you to accomplish tasks is an estimate and may vary greatly per individual. You may want to allow extra time for any distractions that may come up – like hunting down your seam ripper. (Happens to the best of us!)

Squares & Stripes Row Quilt Finished Size: 40" x 52½"	FIRST CUT		SECOND CUT	
	Number of Strips or Pieces	Dimensions	Number of Pieces	Dimensions
Fabric A Large Squares ⅓ yard	1	8" x 42"	3	8" squares
Fabric B Large & Small Squares ⅜ yard	1 1	8" x 42" 3" x 42"	3 1	8" squares 3" x 30"
Fabric C Large Squares & Accent Border ½ yard	1 2	8" x 42" 2½" x 42"	3 2	8" squares 2½" x 38"
Fabric D Large & Small Squares ⅜ yard	1 1	8" x 42" 3" x 42"	3 1	8" squares 3" x 30"
Fabric E Large & Small Squares ⅜ yard	1 1	8" x 42" 3" x 42"	3 1	8" squares 3" x 30"
Fabric F Small Squares ⅙ yard	1	3" x 42"	1	3" x 30"
Fabric G Small Squares ⅙ yard	1	3" x 42"	1	3" x 30"
Fabric H Small Squares ⅙ yard	1	3" x 42"	1	3" x 30"
Fabric I Small Squares & Accent Border ⅝ yard	1 11	3" x 42" 1¼" x 42"	1 2	3" x 30" 1¼" x 38"
Fabric J Accent Border ⅓ yard	6	1¼" x 42"	6	1¼" x 38"
Fabric K Small Squares & Accent Border ⅜ yard	1 6	3" x 42" 1¼" x 42"	1	3" x 30"
Binding ½ yard	5	2¾" x 42"		
Backing - 2⅝ yards Batting - 46" x 59"				

Fabric Requirements and Cutting Instructions

Read all instructions before beginning and use ¼"-wide seam allowances throughout. Read Cutting Strips and Pieces on page 124 prior to cutting fabric.

Getting Started

This simple and quick-to-make quilt features assorted fabrics in an array of colors and textures. Refer to Accurate Seam Allowance on page 124. Whenever possible use Assembly Line Method on page 124. Press seams in direction of arrows.

Making the Quilt

1. Sew lengthwise one 3" x 30" Fabric F strip to one 3" x 30" Fabric D strip as shown to make a strip set. Press seam toward Fabric F. Cut strip set into eight 3" segments.

Cut 8 segments
Press seam toward Fabric F

2. Sew lengthwise one 3" x 30" Fabric B strip to one 3" x 30" Fabric K strip as shown to make a strip set. Press seam toward Fabric K. Cut strip set into eight 3" segments.

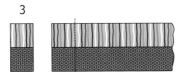

Cut 8 segments
Press seam toward Fabric K

3. Sew lengthwise one 3" x 30" Fabric G strip to one 3" x 30" Fabric E strip as shown to make a strip set. Press seam toward Fabric G. Cut strip set into seven 3" segments.

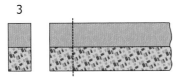

Cut 7 segments
Press seam toward Fabric G

4. Sew lengthwise one 3" x 30" Fabric H strip to one 3" x 30" Fabric I strip as shown to make a strip set. Press seam toward Fabric I. Cut strip set into seven 3" segments.

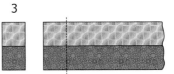

Cut 7 segments
Press seam toward Fabric I

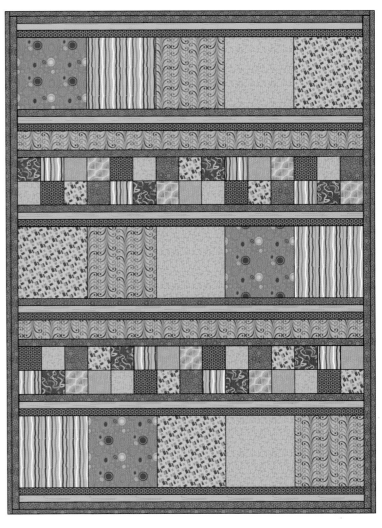

Squares & Stripes
Row Quilt 40" x 52½"

5. Note: Some seams for steps 5 and 6 will need to be repressed so seams fall opposite each other. Arrange and sew together four units from step 1, four units from step 2, three units from step 3, and four units from step 4 as shown. Press.

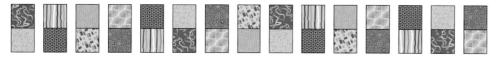

6. Arrange and sew together four units from step 1, four units from step 2, four units from step 3, and three units from step 4 as shown. Press.

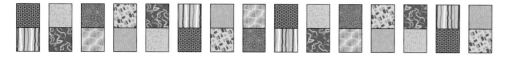

7. Sew lengthwise one 1¼" x 42" Fabric J strip between one 1¼" x 42" Fabric I strip and one 1¼" x 42" Fabric K strip as shown to make a strip set. Press. Make six. Cut strip sets to measure 2¾" x 38".

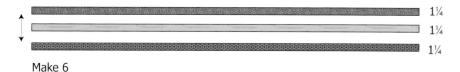

1¼
1¼
1¼

Make 6

8. Arrange and sew together one each of 8" Fabric A, B, C, D, and E squares as shown. Press. Make three, one of each variation.

8   8   8   8   8

8

Make 3
(one of each variation)

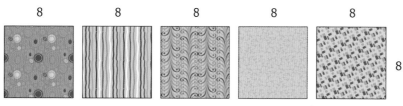

9. Arrange and sew together, six strip sets from step 7, three units from step 8, two 2½" x 38" Fabric C strips, two 1¼" x 38" Fabric I strips, and units from steps 5 and 6 as shown. Press.

38

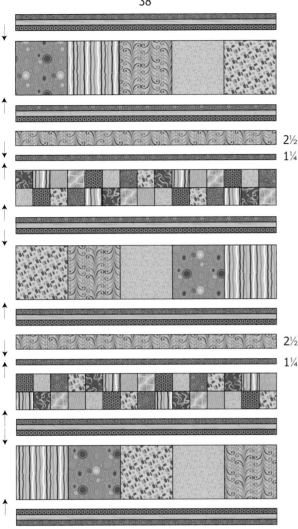

2½
1¼

2½
1¼

10. Sew remaining 1¼" x 42" Fabric I strips together end-to-end to make one continuous 1¼"-wide Fabric I strip. Measure quilt through center from top to bottom. Cut two strips to this measurement. Sew to sides of quilt. Press.

Layering and Finishing

1. Cut backing crosswise into two equal pieces. Sew pieces together lengthwise to make one 47" x 80" (approximate) backing piece. Press and trim to 47" x 60".

2. Referring to Layering the Quilt on page 126, arrange and baste backing, batting, and top together. Hand or machine quilt as desired.

3. Refer to Binding the Quilt on page 126. Sew 2¾" x 42" binding strips end-to-end to make one continuous 2¾"-wide binding strip. Bind quilt to finish.

Squares & Stripes Pillow

Supplies
• • • • • • • •

Appliqué Background - Scrap
  One 6½" square
Accent Squares-Assorted Scraps
  Forty 2½" squares
  (our pillow has six different fabrics)
Border - ⅛ yard
  Two 1" x 15½"
  Two 1" x 14½"
Circles - Assorted Scraps
Backing - ⅜ yard
  Two 10½" x 15½"
Lightweight Fusible Web (18"-wide) - Scraps
Batting & Lining - 19" square each
(Lining doesn't show)
15" Pillow Form

1. Using ¼"-wide seam allowances and referring to photo, arrange and sew together two rows with three 2½" accent squares each. Press seams in opposite directions from row to row. Sew rows together. Press. Make two. Sew one 6½" appliqué background square between these units. Press seams away from background. Arrange and sew together two rows with seven 2½" accent squares each. Sew rows together. Press. Sew to sides of unit. Press.

2. Refer to appliqué instructions on page 125 and circle patterns on page 127 to trace four 2¾" and four 1¾" circles on paper side of fusible web. Use appropriate fabrics to prepare all appliqués for fusing.

3. Refer to photo to position and fuse appliqués to one 6½" appliqué background square. Finish appliqué edges with machine satin stitch or other decorative stitching as desired.

4. Sew unit from step 3 between two 1" x 14½" Border strips. Press seams toward border. Sew unit between two 1" x 15½" Border strips. Press.

5. Referring to Finishing Pillows on page 127, quilt pillow top. Using two 10½" x 15½" backing pieces, sew backing to pillow unit. To create flange, stitch-in-the-ditch between border and pieced top. Insert 15" pillow form or refer to Pillow Forms page 127 to make a pillow form if desired.

Sassy
Log Cabin

1½ DAYS

Weekend Planner

When you only have to coordinate a few different fabrics together for a quilt, it typically will result in speedier sewing because you don't have to spend as much time thinking and planning how you want to place scrap fabrics.
In other words, it's a little more mindless, which is just what the therapist ordered for this weekend project.

SATURDAY MORNING

Hit the fabric store first thing in the morning to pick out just four fabrics that you love together. I went for a contemporary look with modern colors which is reflected in the fabrics I chose. If you are using very trendy patterns and colors, it's a good choice to pick a quick and easy project. That way when the trend has passed you won't have invested as much time and energy in the project.

Head to the drive-through at the coffee stand to get yourself an energy sustainer for your afternoon. Get your cutting done before lunch since it should only take about 45 minutes to an hour.

SATURDAY AFTERNOON

After lunch, you can easily get your blocks pieced in one afternoon. Allow at least 3 hours to complete these.

SUNDAY MORNING

After sleeping in or sipping coffee after church, you'll still have time to piece your top together. You should be able to complete that in about an hour and a half.

SUNDAY AFTERNOON

All that is left to complete your top is to sew the 1" sashing between the rows and finish up the striped borders. This will likely take you a couple hours of devoted straight stitching. Good pressing is critical to keeping these seams looking as straight as possible. Don't forget to keep an eye on your bobbin so it doesn't run out as you stitch up these long border strips.

How long it will take you to accomplish tasks is an estimate and may vary greatly per individual. You may want to allow extra time for any distractions that may come up – like hunting down your seam ripper. (Happens to the best of us!)

Sassy Log Cabin Finished Size: 39½" x 48"	FIRST CUT		SECOND CUT	
	Number of Strips or Pieces	Dimensions	Number of Pieces	Dimensions
Fabric A Block Center ⅜ yard	3	3½" x 42"	24	3½" squares
Fabric B Block 1st Border & Sashing ⅝ yard	3 3 4	2½" x 42" 1½" x 42" 1" x 42"	24 24	2½" x 4½" 1½" x 3½"
Fabric C Block 2nd Border ⅔ yard	1 4 4	3" x 42" 2½" x 42" 1½" x 42"	4 24 24	3" squares 2½" x 5½" 1½" x 5½"
Fabric D Block 3rd Border ¾ yard	5 5	2½" x 42" 1½" x 42"	24 24	2½" x 7½" 1½" x 7½"
Dark Border ½ yard	12	1" x 42"		
Light Border ⅓ yard	8	1" x 42"		
Binding ½ yard	5	2¾" x 42"		
Backing - 2⅝ yards Batting - 46" x 54"				

Fabric Requirements and Cutting Instructions
Read all instructions before beginning and use ¼"-wide seam allowances throughout. Read Cutting Strips and Pieces on page 124 prior to cutting fabric.

Getting Started
This simple and quick-to-make quilt features four fabrics in an array of colors and textures. Refer to Accurate Seam Allowance on page 124. Block measures 8½" x 7½" unfinished. Whenever possible use Assembly Line Method on page 124. Press seams in direction of arrows.

Making the Quilt

1. Sew one 3½" Fabric A square to one 1½" x 3½" Fabric B piece as shown. Press. Make twenty-four.

3½

3½

1½

Make 24

2. Sew one unit from step 1 to one 2½" x 4½" Fabric B piece as shown. Press. Make twenty-four.

2½

4½

Make 24

3. Sew one 1½" x 5½" Fabric C piece to one unit from step 2 as shown. Press. Make twenty-four.

5½

1½

Make 24

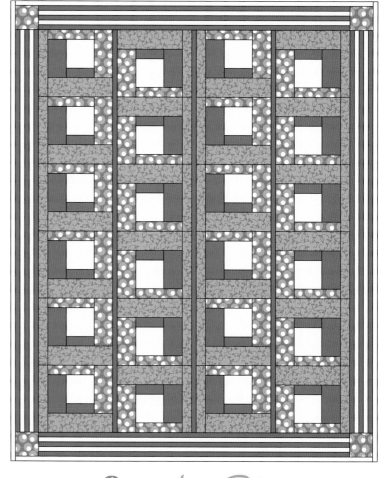

Sassy Log Cabin
39½" x 48"

4. Sew one 2½" x 5½" Fabric C piece to one unit from step 3 as shown. Press. Make twenty-four.

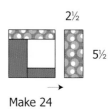

2½

5½

Make 24

5. Sew one 2½" x 7½" Fabric D piece to one unit from step 4 as shown. Press. Make twenty-four.

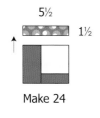

7½

2½

Make 24

52

6. Sew one 1½" x 7½" Fabric D piece to one unit from step 5 as shown. Press half as shown and half in the opposite direction. Make twenty-four. Block measures 8½" x 7½".

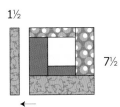

Make 24
(Press half in the opposite direction)
Block measures 8½" x 7½"

Assembling and Adding the Borders

1. Arrange and sew together six blocks as shown. Press. Make four.

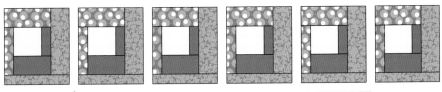

Make 4

2. Sew 1" x 42" Fabric B strips together end-to-end to make one continuous 1"-wide Fabric B strip. Measure row length from step 1 and cut three 1"-wide Fabric B strips to this measurement. Note: Prior to sewing strips together, check length of Fabric B strips. If there is 42½" usable length, you don't need to sew strips together.

3. Referring to layout on page 52, arrange and sew together four rows from step 1 and three 1"-wide Fabric B strips from step 2. Press seams toward Fabric B.

4. Measure quilt from side to side and cut six 1" x 42" Dark Border strips to this measurement. Sew remaining 1" x 42" Dark Border strips together end-to-end to make one continuous 1"-wide Dark Border strip. Measure quilt through center from top to bottom and cut six 1"-wide strips to this measurement.

5. Repeat step 4 to sew and cut four 1"-wide Light Border strips to width measurement and four 1"-wide strips to length measurement.

6. Sew three shorter Dark Border strips and two shorter Light Border strips together. Press seams toward dark fabric. Make two. Sew to top and bottom of quilt. Press seams toward border unit.

7. Sew three remaining Dark Border strips and two remaining Light Border strips together. Press seams toward dark fabric. Make two.

8. Sew one border unit from step 7 between two 3" Fabric C squares as shown. Press. Make two. Sew to sides of quilt. Press.

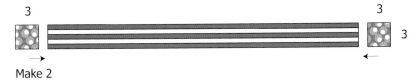

Make 2

Layering and Finishing

1. Cut backing into two equal pieces. Sew pieces together lengthwise to make one 47" x 80" (approximate) backing piece. Press and trim to 47" x 54".

2. Referring to Layering the Quilt on page 126, arrange and baste backing, batting, and top together. Hand or machine quilt as desired.

3. Refer to Binding the Quilt on page 126. Sew 2¾" x 42" binding strips end-to-end to make one continuous 2¾"-wide binding strip. Bind quilt to finish.

Retro
Table Quilt

1
DAY

Weekend Planner

You may be detecting a trend of one of my favorite color stories for this book, and if you guessed green, turquoise and taupe, you'd be absolutely correct. When you do this project, you will be so happy later if you pick up a circle template at the art store. Tracing your circles will be slicker than you could have imagined.

SATURDAY MORNING

A three-color fabric story is the perfect combination for this table topper quilt. Once again this is a perfect opportunity to use fabric scraps, eighth-yard cuts and fat quarters to put this project together. Cutting and piecing the background blocks will be lickity-split quick — less than an hour! Prep all appliqué pieces for sewing over the following hour. For easy placement, position the four larger circles at the center point of each of the large square blocks (approximately ¾" from the fabric edge) and then center the smaller circles between them.

SATURDAY AFTERNOON

Coordinate your appliqué thread colors to your fabric circles and spend an hour or so zigzagging your way around all the circles. In the next 45 minutes you can quickly piece the blocks together and add the border. After quilting, add "Big Stitch" embroidery to create the look of a kitschy dingbat shape — it's funky and fun for sure!

How long it will take you to accomplish tasks is an estimate and may vary greatly per individual. You may want to allow extra time for any distractions that may come up – like hunting down your seam ripper. (Happens to the best of us!)

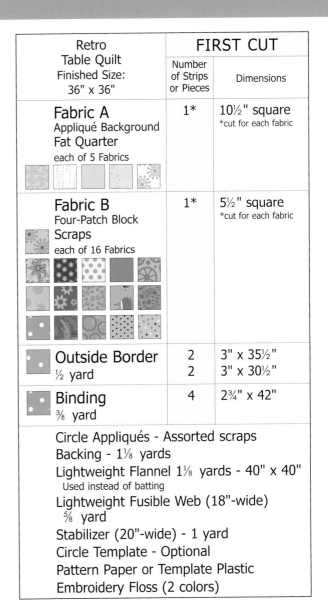

Retro Table Quilt Finished Size: 36" x 36"	FIRST CUT	
	Number of Strips or Pieces	Dimensions
Fabric A Appliqué Background Fat Quarter each of 5 Fabrics	1*	10½" square *cut for each fabric
Fabric B Four-Patch Block Scraps each of 16 Fabrics	1*	5½" square *cut for each fabric
Outside Border ½ yard	2 2	3" x 35½" 3" x 30½"
Binding ⅜ yard	4	2¾" x 42"

Circle Appliqués - Assorted scraps
Backing - 1⅛ yards
Lightweight Flannel 1⅛ yards - 40" x 40"
  Used instead of batting
Lightweight Fusible Web (18"-wide)
  ⅝ yard
Stabilizer (20"-wide) - 1 yard
Circle Template - Optional
Pattern Paper or Template Plastic
Embroidery Floss (2 colors)

Fabric Requirements and Cutting Instructions

Read all instructions before beginning and use ¼"-wide seam allowances throughout. Read Cutting Strips and Pieces on page 124 prior to cutting fabric.

Getting Started
Adorn your table with a touch from the past with a contemporary flair. Block measures 10½" square (unfinished). Refer to Accurate Seam Allowance on page 124. Whenever possible use Assembly Line Method on page 124. Press seams in direction of arrows.

Adding the Appliqués

Refer to appliqué instructions on page 125. Our instructions are for Quick-Fuse Appliqué, but if you prefer hand appliqué, add ¼"-wide seam allowances.

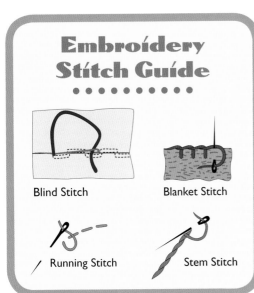

Embroidery Stitch Guide

Blind Stitch   Blanket Stitch

Running Stitch   Stem Stitch

1. To aid in aligning circles make a placement template. Draw a 10" square on pattern paper or template plastic. Draw lines as shown dividing square in half vertically and horizontally, and drawing diagonal lines from corner to corner. Refer to page 127 to trace an 8" circle in the center. Cut out circle on drawn line.

Placement Template

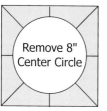

2. Use patterns on pages 127 to trace twenty 2½" circles and twenty 2" circles on paper side of fusible web. Use appropriate fabrics to prepare all appliqués for fusing.

3. Using placement template from step 1, and referring to photo on page 54 and layout, position eight circles, four of each size on one 10½" Fabric A square. Place template on top of circles to evenly space them on the square. Fuse in place. Finish appliqué edges with machine satin stitch or other decorative stitching as desired. Make five Appliqué Blocks.

Making the Quilt

1. Sew two different 5½" Fabric B squares together as shown. Press. Make eight in assorted fabric combinations. Sew two of these units together to make a Four-Patch block. Refer to Twisting Seams on page 124. Press. Make four. Block measures 10½" square.

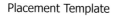

Make 8
(in assorted fabric combinations)

Make 4
(in assorted fabric combinations)

2. Sew one Four-Patch block from step 1 between two Appliqué blocks as shown. Press. Make two.

Make 2

3. Sew one Appliqué block between two Four-Patch blocks from step 1 as shown. Press.

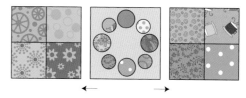

4. Referring to photo on page 54 and layout below, sew row from step 3 between two rows from step 2. Press.

5. Sew two 3" x 30½" Outside Border strips to sides of top from step 4. Press toward border. Sew two 3" x 35½" Outside Border strips to top and bottom of quilt. Press.

Layering and Finishing

This quilt has lightweight flannel instead of batting so the finished piece drapes nicely.

1. Referring to Layering the Quilt on page 126, arrange and baste backing, lightweight flannel, and top together. Hand or machine quilt as desired.

2. Refer to Binding the Quilt on page 126. Use 2¾"-wide Binding strips to bind quilt.

3. Referring to photo on page 54 and layout, mark lines, with removable fabric marker, across center of block. Using six strands of embroidery floss and a long running stitch, sew on the marked lines to create center design.

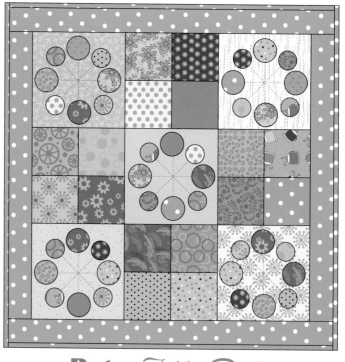

Retro Table Quilt
36" x 36"

Vintage Flowers
Wall Quilt

1 DAY

57

Weekend Planner

I have a soft spot in my heart for vintage styled projects, but I'm not a fan of the intricate piecing that's needed to make a Grandmother's flower garden. My simple solution is to do appliquéd circles. It's quick and old-fashioned looking. With bright, clean colors you can also achieve the look of pop art that would be cute for a girl's bedroom.

FRIDAY EVENING

Choose your fabrics tonight. Sort through and select possible fabrics from your bin. I repeated some of the background fabrics in the border, however each of my flowers fabrics and four-patch background fabrics are all different. This can bring out that "charm" quality to your wall quilt. Make this project with friends and you can share your scraps with each other. Look for an assortment of soft colors to mimic the vintage look.

SATURDAY MORNING

Start your day with an old-fashioned breakfast of eggs, bacon, and jellied toast so you'll be nourished and ready to go. Head out to pick up whatever fabrics you need to round out your selection of scrap fabrics. Even though I used all different fabrics, don't feel that is necessary. You will still achieve a scrappy look even if you prefer to repeat some of your fabrics. In addition to picking up fabrics, make time to run by an art supply store to purchase a circle template. These templates have multiple sizes of circles and are so handy to have around!

Spend the next hour cutting your pieces for the background and border. Piecing the four background blocks will be super-fast — knock it out in less than 30 minutes after you decide how to place fabrics.

SATURDAY AFTERNOON

Allow about an hour to fuse your small and large flower circles onto fusible web. Fuse circles to your scrap fabrics, and cut them out. I usually do a few extra in case I change my mind on a couple of my fabric choices. Press each flower block and plan to spend the next hour appliquéing them in place. (In this case I used the same medium taupe color thread for all the flower petal appliques which is much quicker than changing thread color for every different color petal.) Grab a late afternoon cup of coffee and some cookies before you wrap up your last hour piecing the blocks together and attach the simple pieced border. Awe, so sweet!

How long it will take you to accomplish tasks is an estimate and may vary greatly per individual. You may want to allow extra time for any distractions that may come up – like hunting down your seam ripper. (Happens to the best of us!)

Vintage Flowers Wall Qult Finished Size: 26" x 26"	FIRST CUT		SECOND CUT	
	Number of Strips or Pieces	Dimensions	Number of Pieces	Dimensions
Background Scraps each of 16 Fabrics	1*	5½" square *cut for each fabric		
First Border ⅛ yard	4	1" x 42"	2 2	1" x 21½" 1" x 20½"
Outside Border Assorted scraps	6** 4** 8** 12**	2½" x 4½" 2½" x 4" 2½" x 3½" 2½" x 3"		
4½" Circle Appliqués Assorted scraps	4**	5½" squares		
2½" Circle Appliqués Assorted scraps	28**	3½" squares		
Binding ⅜ yard	4	2¾" x 42"		
Backing - ⅞ yard Batting - 30" x 30" Lightweight Fusible Web (18"-wide) - ¾ yard Stabilizer (20"-wide) - ⅔ yard Circle Template (Optional) **Total needed for quilt - cut from assorted fabrics.				

Fabric Requirements and Cutting Instructions
Read all instructions before beginning and use ¼"-wide seam allowances throughout. Read Cutting Strips and Pieces on page 124 prior to cutting fabric.

Getting Started
This quilt is truly a scrappy quilt with only the First Border requiring yardage. The repeating block consists of four different fabric squares, a large flower center and small flower blossoms. Block measures 10½" square (unfinished). Refer to Accurate Seam Allowance on page 124. Whenever possible use Assembly Line Method on page 124. Press seams in direction of arrows.

Making the Block

Refer to appliqué instructions on page 125. Our instructions are for Quick-Fuse Appliqué, but if you prefer hand appliqué, add ¼"-wide seam allowances.

1. Sew two different 5½" Background squares together as shown. Press. Make eight in assorted fabric combinations. Sew two of these units together. Refer to Twisting Seams on page 124. Press. Make four.

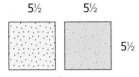

Make 8
(in assorted fabric combinations)

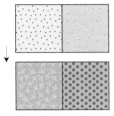

Make 4
(in assorted fabric combinations)

2. Use pattern on pages 127 to make templates and trace four 4½" circles and twenty-eight 2½" circles on paper side of fusible web. Use appropriate fabrics to prepare all appliqués for fusing.

3. Refer to photo on page 57 and layout to position and fuse appliqués to block from step 1. Finish appliqué edges with machine satin stitch or other decorative stitching as desired.

Assembling the Quilt

1. Arrange and sew together two rows with two blocks each. Press seams in opposite direction from row to row. Sew rows together. Press.

2. Sew two 1" x 20½" First Border strips to top and bottom of quilt. Press seams toward border. Sew two 1" x 21½" First Border strips to sides of quilt. Press.

3. Using assorted fabrics, arrange and sew together three 2½" x 3", one 2½" x 4", two 2½" x 3½", and one 2½" x 4½" Outside Border pieces as shown. Press. Make two. Sew units to sides of quilt. Press.

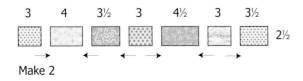

Make 2

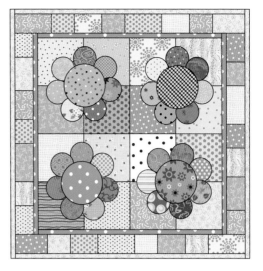

Vintage Flowers
Wall Quilt 26" x 26"

4. Using assorted fabrics, arrange and sew together two 2½" x 4½", three 2½" x 3", two 2½" x 3½", and one 2½" x 4" Outside Border pieces as shown. Press. Make two. Sew units to top and bottom of quilt.

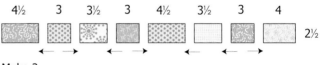

Make 2

Layering and Finishing

1. Referring to Layering the Quilt on page 126, arrange and baste backing, batting, and top together. Hand or machine quilt as desired.

2. Refer to Binding the Quilt on page 126. Use 2¾"-wide binding strips to bind quilt.

Vintage Bird
Wall Art

1 DAY

Weekend Planner

Love these sweet quickie projects! This is really a scrap fabric project because the pieces for this one are so small.

SATURDAY MORNING

If you don't have the right fabrics, you may need to spend your morning out on the hunt to pick up some obese (or regular cut) eighths to make this project. I love the vintage quality that you get from old fashioned and soft hued fabrics. Keeping the background fabrics low key, but with interesting texture, will make sure the birds stand out. The little sparkle of the milky orange, soft yellow and turquoise keeps it fun and nostalgic. Sometimes picking fabrics for these little projects can take a surprising amount of time (at least that's my "M.O.").

SATURDAY AFTERNOON

You can knock out cutting and piecing the background in about 30 to 45 minutes. Since you've already chosen your fabrics – tracing, fusing and cutting your appliqué pieces will be a snap – 30 minutes tops. (unless you do some more fussing!) Allow an additional 45 more minutes to do your appliqué stitching.
It will likely take you another 1 – 2 hours to complete some simple machine quilting and to add the binding. If you choose to use a wire hanger like I did, you will also need to make up a sleeve to attach the hanger. Allow another 30 minutes for that process.

Wire hanger is from Ackfeld Wire.
Check out their assortment of wire hangers at www.ackfeldwire.com

How long it will take you to accomplish tasks is an estimate and may vary greatly per individual. You may want to allow extra time for any distractions that may come up – like hunting down your seam ripper. (Happens to the best of us!)

Vintage Bird Wall Art Finished Size: 7½" x 18"	FIRST CUT	
	Number of Strips or Pieces	Dimensions
Fabric A Background & Top Binding Obese Eighth	1	7½" x 7"
	1	2½" x 12"
Fabric B Background Scrap	1	7½" x 6⅝"
Fabric C Background Scrap	1	7½" x 6⅞"
Fabric D Background Scrap	1	7½" x 4"
Fabric E Accents Scrap each of 3 Fabrics	1*	1" x 10" *cut for each fabric
Binding ¼ yard	2	2½" x 42" ¼" finished binding

Appliqués - Assorted scraps
Backing - ⅓ yard
Batting - 12" x 22"
Lightweight Fusible Web (18"-wide) ½ yard
Stabilizer (20"-wide) - ⅓ yard
⅛" Buttons - 4
Wire Hanger - Optional

Fabric Requirements and Cutting Instructions

Read all instructions before beginning and use ¼"-wide seam allowances throughout. Read Cutting Strips and Pieces on page 124 prior to cutting fabric.

Getting Started
This whimsical quilt is fun to make and wonderful to gaze at with its playful angles and sweet birds. Refer to Accurate Seam Allowance on page 124. Whenever possible use Assembly Line Method on page 124. Press seams in direction of arrows.

Making the Quilt

This quilt has odd angles that need to be cut prior to sewing. Refer to diagram below to mark and cut fabric pieces. Note: All background pieces are marked on the right side of fabric.

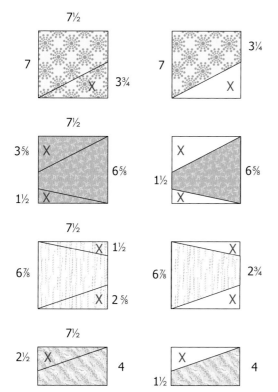

Mark right side of all fabrics.
X-Remove pieces, not used in quilt

Vintage Bird
Wall Art 7½" x 24½"

1. Mark 7½" x 7" Fabric A piece 3¼" from top right side, draw line from this mark to left bottom corner. Cut on drawn line. Top section is used in quilt.

2. Mark 7½" x 6⅝" Fabric B piece 3⅝" down from top left corner, draw a line from this mark to top right corner. Mark 1½" up from bottom left corner, draw a line from this mark to bottom right corner. Cut on drawn lines. Center section is used in quilt.

3. Mark 7½" x 6⅞" Fabric C piece 1½" down from right top corner, draw a line from this mark to top left corner. Mark 2⅝" up from bottom right corner, draw a line from this mark to bottom left corner. Cut on drawn lines. Center section is used in quilt.

4. Mark 7½" x 4" Fabric D piece 2½" from top left corner, draw line from this mark to top right corner. Cut on drawn line. Bottom section is used in quilt.

5. Arrange and sew together cut pieces from steps 1-4 and three 1" x 10" Fabric E pieces as shown. Press. Trim excess Fabric E pieces to match sides of quilt. NOTE: When sewing sections together, align side edges of large pieces to keep quilt straight along sides. Sew Fabric E to larger piece then trim before sewing next piece.

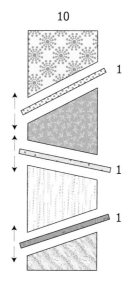

Adding the Appliqués

Refer to appliqué instructions on page 125. Our instructions are for Quick-Fuse Appliqué, but if you prefer hand appliqué, reverse patterns and add ¼"-wide seam allowances.

1. Use patterns on page 63 to trace three birds, one of each, on paper side of fusible web. Use appropriate fabrics to prepare all appliqués for fusing.

2. Refer to photo on page 60 and layout above to position and fuse appliqués to quilt. Finish appliqué edges with machine satin stitch or other decorative stitching as desired.

Layering and Finishing the Quilt

1. Referring to Layering the Quilt on page 126, arrange and baste backing, batting, and top together. Hand or machine quilt as desired.

2. Refer to Binding the Quilt on page 126. Use 2¼"-wide binding strips to bind quilt. Note: Finished width of binding is ¼" instead of our normal ½".

3. Referring to photo on page 60 and patterns, sew one or two buttons on each bird for eyes.

4. To make a hanging sleeve, cut one 3" x 8" backing fabric piece. Fold one short side ¼" to the wrong side and press. Fold piece again ¼", press, and stitch along folded edges. Repeat for other short side.

5. Fold unit from step 4 in half lengthwise, right sides together, and stitch. Turn unit right side out centering seam and press.

6. Hanging sleeve covers part of binding. Center hanging sleeve on backside of quilt along top edge with seam of sleeve against quilt. Hand-stitch top and bottom sleeve edges leaving short ends free of stitching.

Vintage Bird Wall Art
Patterns are reversed for use with Quick-Fuse Appliqué (page 125)

Tracing Line _____
Tracing Line - - - - - - - - - - - - - - - -
(will be hidden behind other fabrics)

Símple Geometry
Wall Art Quilt

1½ DAYS

Weekend Planner

So simple, yet so striking! I love the way the design creates dimensional layering. I created this to appeal to the modern decorator. I also think it would be stunning wrapped over stretcher bars which would really emphasize this as a piece of wall art.

SATURDAY MORNING

Because this is simple piecing with fewer blocks, you don't need to get your fabrics prior to the weekend to be done by Sunday evening. This is essentially a three hue color story. Mine consists of three turquoises, two grays and three tan/taupes. The colors you go with will determine how modern and trendy your quilt will be. Enjoy your morning of designing your own color story.

SATURDAY AFTERNOON

Cutting your strips and pieces can be done in an hour. The simplicity of this design may be slightly deceiving since there are actually three different blocks to keep track of. So it is essential to organize your fabrics before you start piecing your blocks. Once you're prepared, the block piecing will take you about an hour and a half. Allow another half an hour to piece the turquoise borders around each block.

SUNDAY MORNING

You certainly could have finished this up on Saturday if you were determined. However, if you're not rushing – you are less likely to make mistakes, which always eat a lot of time! Do a double check to make sure everything is in the right position and take half an hour to sew the nine blocks together. Adding your two borders adds about another 30 minutes. The rest of your day is left for other activities!

How long it will take you to accomplish tasks is an estimate and may vary greatly per individual. You may want to allow extra time for any distractions that may come up – like hunting down your seam ripper. *(Happens to the best of us!)*

Simple Geometry Wall Art Quilt Finished Size: 35" x 35"	FIRST CUT		SECOND CUT	
	Number of Strips or Pieces	Dimensions	Number of Pieces	Dimensions
Fabric A Block Square Fat Eighth	8	3½" squares		
Fabric B Block Square Fat Eighth	8	3½" squares		
Fabric C Block Accent Border ⅙ yard	2	1½" x 42"	8 8	1½" x 4½" 1½" x 3½"
Fabric D Block Accent Border ⅙ yard	2	1½" x 42"	8 8	1½" x 4½" 1½" x 3½"
Fabric E Block Outside Border ¼ yard	3	1½" x 42"	6 6	1½" x 10½" 1½" x 8½"
Fabric F Block Outside Border ¼ yard	3	1½" x 42"	6 6	1½" x 10½" 1½" x 8½"
Fabric G Block Outside Border ¼ yard	3	1½" x 42"	6 6	1½" x 10½" 1½" x 8½"
Fabric H Background ½ yard	3	4½" x 42"	8 4	4½" x 8½" 4½" squares
First Border ⅙ yard	4	1" x 42"	2 2	1" x 31½" 1" x 30½"
Outside Border ⅓ yard	4	2" x 42"	2 2	2" x 34½" 2" x 31½"
Binding ⅜ yard	4	2¾" x 42"		
Backing - 1⅛ yards Batting - 39" x 39"				

Fabric Requirements and Cutting Instructions Read all instructions before beginning and use ¼"-wide seam allowances throughout. Read Cutting Strips and Pieces on page 124 prior to cutting fabric.

Getting Started This quilt has the illusion of depth with its squares on top of squares design. It's a great quilt for beginners with its easy-to-construct techniques. Block measures 10½" square (unfinished). Refer to Accurate Seam Allowance on page 124. Whenever possible use Assembly Line Method on page 124. Press seams in direction of arrows.

Making and Assembling the Quilt

Note: Pay close attention to orientation of blocks in steps 8-10. Place all units as shown in diagrams. When sewing borders on blocks, blocks are oriented so seams will be in opposite direction when sewing blocks and rows together.

1. Sew one 1½" x 3½" Fabric C piece to one 3½" Fabric A square as shown. Press. Sew one 1½" x 4½" Fabric C piece to unit from this step. Press. Make eight.

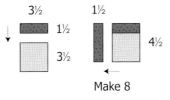

Make 8

2. Sew one 4½" Fabric H square to one unit from step 1 as shown. Press. Sew one 4½" x 8½" Fabric H piece to unit from this step. Press. Make two and label Unit 1.

Unit 1

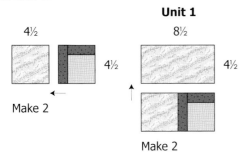

Make 2

Make 2

3. Sew one 1½" x 3½" Fabric D piece to one 3½" Fabric B square as shown. Press. Sew one 1½" x 4½" Fabric D piece to this unit. Press. Make eight.

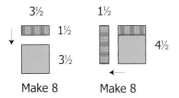

Make 8   Make 8

4. Sew one 4½" Fabric H square to one unit from step 3 as shown. Press. Sew one 4½" x 8½" Fabric H piece to unit from this step. Press. Make two and label Unit 2.

Unit 2

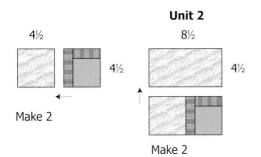

Make 2

Make 2

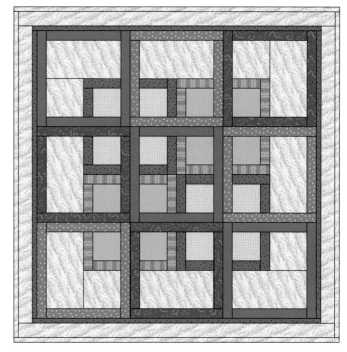

Simple Geometry
Wall Art Quilt 35" x 35"

5. Sew one unit from step 1 to one unit from step 3 as shown. Press. Make two. Sew one 4½" x 8½" Fabric H piece to unit from this step. Press. Make two and label Unit 3.

Unit 3

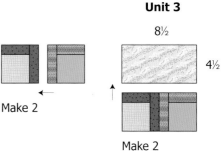

Make 2

Make 2

6. Sew one unit from step 3 to one unit from step 1 as shown. Press. Make four. Sew one 4½" x 8½" Fabric H piece to one unit from this step. Press. Make two and label Unit 4.

Unit 4

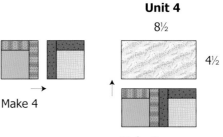

Make 4

Make 2

7. Sew two remaining units from step 6 together as shown. Press and label Unit 5.

Unit 5

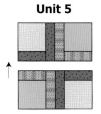

8. Sew one Unit 3 between two 1½" x 8½" Fabric E pieces. Press seams toward Fabric E. Sew this unit between two 1½" x 10½" Fabric E pieces as shown noting block orientation. (Row 1 Block 2). Press. Repeat to sew borders to one Unit 4 (Row 2 Block 3) and one Unit 2 (Row 3 Block 1).

1½   1½

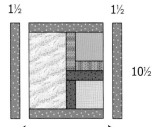

10½

Row 1 Block 2
Block measures 10½" square

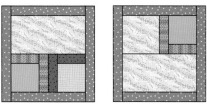

Row 2 Block 3   Row 3 Block 1

9. Sew one Unit 2 between two 1½" x 8½" Fabric F pieces. Press seams toward Fabric F. Sew this unit between two 1½" x 10½" Fabric F pieces as shown noting block orientation. (Row 1 Block 3). Press. Repeat to sew borders to one Unit 4 (Row 2 Block 1) and one Unit 3 (Row 3 Block 2).

1½   1½

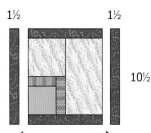

10½

Row 1 Block 3
Block measures 10½" square

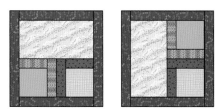

Row 2 Block 1   Row 3 Block 2

10. Sew one Unit 1 between two 1½" x 8½" Fabric G pieces. Press seams toward Fabric G. Sew this unit between two 1½" x 10½" Fabric G pieces as shown noting block orientation. (Row 1 Block 1). Press. Repeat to sew borders to one Unit 5 (Row 2 Block 2) and one Unit 1 (Row 3 Block 3).

1½   1½

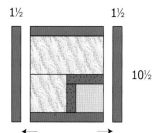

10½

Row 1 Block 1
Block measures 10½" square

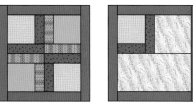

Row 2 Block 2   Row 3 Block 3

11. Referring to photo on page 64 and layout on page 66, arrange blocks into three rows with three blocks each. Sew blocks into rows pressing seams in opposite direction from row to row. Sew rows together. Press.

Adding the Borders

1. Sew two 1" x 30½" First Border strips to sides of quilt. Press seams toward border. Sew 1" x 31½" First Border to top and bottom of quilt. Press.

2. Sew two 2" x 31½" Outside Border strips to sides of quilt. Press seams toward border just sewn. Sew 2" x 34½" Outside Border strips to top and bottom of quilt. Press.

Layering and Finishing

1. Referring to Layering the Quilt on page 126, arrange and baste backing, batting, and top together. Hand or machine quilt as desired.

2. Refer to Binding the Quilt on page 126. Use 2¾"-wide binding strips to bind quilt.

Take it Easy Quilt

1½ DAYS

Weekend Planner

This project will not stress you out like some complicated quilt designs can. In fact you can take it easy this weekend and still get this darling quilt top completed. Four very simple geometric patterns create the centers of these square blocks.

SATURDAY MORNING

When you take this pattern out with you shopping, you can follow my lead by purchasing a variety of scales of prints. Depending on where you cut your pieces from the larger scale prints, it can give a different look, which can make it look like there are even more fabrics being used than there actually are. I went trendy with a gray and coral color combination, but naturally you can always take any project any color direction that you desire.

SATURDAY AFTERNOON

Once you've finalized your plan for what fabric goes where, then you can spend the next 45 minutes cutting your pieces. Then start your piecing. It's always more time efficient to repeat the same step until it is completed, and then move to the next step. For instance, do all the four-patch centers before moving on to the four strip centers, etc. Plan on a good couple of hours to complete blocks.

SUNDAY AFTERNOON

Part of the "Take it Easy" plan is to spend a very relaxing morning, but after lunch it's time to gather your blocks and lay them out. Put one of each block combination in each row. Block out the next two hours for piecing your blocks together and adding the borders.

How long it will take you to accomplish tasks is an estimate and may vary greatly per individual. You may want to allow extra time for any distractions that may come up – like hunting down your seam ripper. (Happens to the best of us!)

Take it Easy Quilt Finished Size: 40" x 48"	FIRST CUT		SECOND CUT	
	Number of Strips or Pieces	Dimensions	Number of Pieces	Dimensions
Fabric A Block 1 Outside Border, Block 2 Strip & Block 4 Accent Squares ½ yard	4	2½" x 42"	10	2½" x 8½"
			10	2½" x 4½"
	2	1½" x 42"	5	1½" x 4½"
			20	1½" squares
Fabric B Block 2 Outside Border ⅓ yard	4	2½" x 42"	10	2½" x 8½"
			10	2½" x 4½"
Fabric C Block 1 Four-Patch, Block 3 Accent Border & Block 4 Outside Border ½ yard	5	2½" x 42"	10	2½" x 8½"
			10	2½" x 4½"
			10	2½" squares
	2	1½" x 42"	10	1½" x 4½"
			10	1½" x 2½"
Fabric D Block 2 Strip & Block 3 Outside Border ⅜ yard	4	2½" x 42"	10	2½" x 8½"
			10	2½" x 4½"
	1	1½" x 42"	5	1½" x 4½"
Fabric E Block 2 Strip & Block 4 Center ⅛ yard	1	2½" x 42"	5	2½" squares
			5	1½" x 4½"
Fabric F Block 2 Strip & Block 3 Center ⅛ yard	1	2½" x 42"	5	2½" squares
			5	1½" x 4½"
Fabric G Block 1 Four-Patch & Block 4 1st Border ¼ yard	1	2½" x 42"	10	2½" squares
	2	1½" x 42"	20	1½" x 2½"
First Border ¼ yard	5	1" x 42"		
Second Border ¼ yard	5	1" x 42"		
Outside Border ½ yard	5	3" x 42"		
Binding ½ yard	5	2¾" x 42"		

Backing - 1½ yards (fabric must be at least 44"-wide) or 2½ yards pieced
Batting - 44" x 52"

Fabric Requirements and Cutting Instructions
Read all instructions before beginning and use ¼"-wide seam allowances throughout. Read Cutting Strips and Pieces on page 124 prior to cutting fabric.

Getting Started
Variety is the spice of life and these blocks fit the bill by featuring four different center pieced units. Block measures 8½" square (unfinished). Refer to Accurate Seam Allowance on page 124. Whenever possible use Assembly Line Method on page 124. Press seams in direction of arrows.

Making the Blocks

1. Sew one 2½" Fabric C square to one 2½" Fabric G square as shown. Press. Make ten. Sew two units together. Refer to Twisting Seams on page 124. Press. Make five.

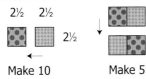

2½   2½   2½

Make 10   Make 5

2. Sew one unit from step 1 between two 2½" x 4½" Fabric A pieces as shown. Press. Make five.

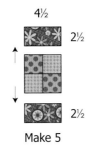

4½
2½
2½

Make 5

3. Sew one unit from step 2 between two 2½" x 8½" Fabric A pieces as shown. Press. Make five and label Block 1. Block measures 8½" square.

Block 1
2½   2½

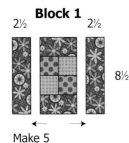

8½

Make 5
Block meausres 8½" square

4. Arrange and sew together one 1½" x 4½" Fabric A piece, one 1½" x 4½" Fabric E piece, one 1½" x 4½" Fabric F piece, and one 1½" x 4½" Fabric D piece as shown. Press. Make five.

1½ 1½ 1½ 1½

4½

Make 5

5. Sew one unit from step 4 between two 2½" x 4½" Fabric B pieces as shown. Press. Make five.

4½
2½

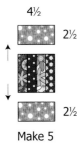

2½

Make 5

6. Sew one unit from step 5 between two 2½" x 8½" Fabric B pieces as shown. Press. Make five and label Block 2. Block measures 8½" square.

Block 2
2½   2½

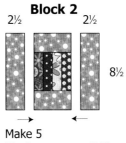

8½

Make 5
Block meausres 8½" square

7. Sew one 2½" Fabric F square between two 1½" x 2½" Fabric C pieces as shown. Press. Make five. Sew this unit between two 1½" x 4½" Fabric C pieces. Press. Make five.

1½ 2½ 1½   4½
                        1½
2½   1½

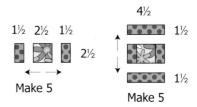

Make 5   Make 5

8. Sew one unit from step 7 between two 2½" x 4½" Fabric D pieces as shown. Press. Make five.

4½
2½

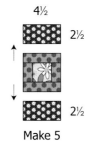

2½

Make 5

9. Sew one unit from step 8 between two 2½" x 8½" Fabric D pieces as shown. Press. Make five and label Block 3. Block measures 8½" square.

Block 3
2½   2½

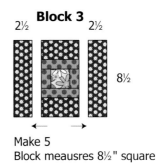

8½

Make 5
Block meausres 8½" square

10. Sew one 1½" x 2½" Fabric G piece between two 1½" Fabric A pieces as shown. Make ten.

1½ 2½ 1½
1½

Make 10

11. Sew one 2½" Fabric E square between two 1½" x 2½" Fabric G pieces as shown. Make five.

1½ 2½ 1½

2½

Make 5

12. Sew one unit from step 11 between two units from step 10 as shown. Press. Make five.

Make 5

13. Sew one unit from step 12 between two 2½" x 4½" Fabric C pieces as shown. Press. Make five.

4½

2½

2½

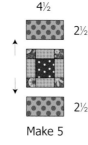

Make 5

14. Sew one unit from step 13 between two 2½" x 8½" Fabric C pieces as shown. Press. Make five and label Block 4. Block measures 8½" square.

Block 4

2½   2½

8½

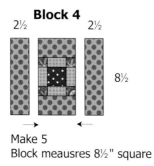

Make 5
Block meausres 8½" square

Assembling and Adding the Borders

1. Referring to layout above, arrange blocks into five rows, with four blocks each. Each row contains one of each block variation.

2. Sew blocks into rows. Some blocks seams may need to be pressed in the opposite direction depending on block orientation. Press seams in opposite direction from row to row. Sew rows together. Press

3. Measure quilt through center from top to bottom. Cut two 1"-wide First Border strips to this measurement. Sew to sides of quilt. Press.

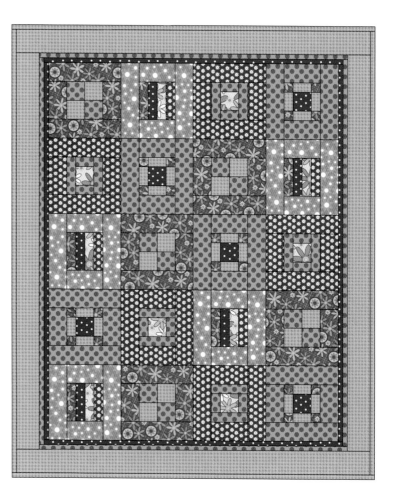

Take it Easy Quilt
40" x 48"

4. Measure quilt through center from side to side including borders just added. Cut two 1"-wide First Border strips to this measurement. Sew to top and bottom of quilt. Press seams toward border.

5. Refer to steps 3 and 4 to join, measure, trim, and sew 1"-wide Second Border strips and 3"-wide Outside Border strips to sides, top, and bottom of quilt. Press.

Layering and Finishing

1. Referring to Layering the Quilt on page 126, arrange and baste backing, batting, and top together. Hand or machine quilt as desired.

2. Refer to Binding the Quilt on page 126. Sew 2¾" x 42" binding strips end-to-end to make one continuous 2¾"-wide binding strip. Bind quilt to finish.

Kitchen Cuties
Ensemble

2 DAYS

72

Apron

See cutting chart on page 74.

1. For Pocket: Sew 4½" x 5½" Fabric D piece between one 3" x 5½" Fabric B piece and one 1½" x 5½" Fabric C piece. Press seams toward Fabric D.

2. Trace pocket-lining pattern and placement lines on page 75 onto pattern paper or template plastic. Cut on drawn line to make pattern.

3. Using pattern from step 2, trace pattern, including placement lines, on wrong side of 5½" x 8" Fabric B piece. Cut on drawn outside line.

4. Place lining piece and pocket unit from step 1 right sides together, aligning placement lines with seam lines. Using ¼"-wide seam, stitch around all edges, leaving a 2" opening on one side for turning. Trim pocket unit even with lining edges. Clip corners, turn, and press. Hand-stitch opening closed. Referring to photo, fold top edge down to form pocket flap. Press. Sew button to flap, stitching through all layers.

5. Position pocket on 15" x 31" Fabric A piece and pin in place. Note: Fabric A will be gathered to measure 20" in width; adjust pocket placement accordingly. Topstitch pocket to apron along sides and bottom edges.

6. Narrow hem sides of apron from step 5 by turning side edge ¼" inch to the wrong side. Press. Fold side edge again to wrong side, press, and stitch along edge. Repeat for opposite side. Optional: Some sewing machines come with a rolled hem foot. Make narrow side hems using foot and following manufacturer's instructions.

7. Mark center top and center bottom along 31" side of Fabric A. Sew basting stitch (longest straight stitch setting on sewing machine) ¼" and ⅛" from top raw edge. Pull bobbin threads to gather skirt to measure 20", making sure gathers are even on both halves of skirt. Optional: If sewing machine has a gathering foot, follow manufacturer's instruction to gather fabric to measure 20".

8. Sew 4½" x 40" Fabric C strips together end-to-end to make one continuous 4½"-wide Fabric C strip. Cut strip to measure 4½" x 79½". On wrong side of fabric mark center.

9. Place gathered unit from step 7 on Fabric C strip from step 8 right sides together matching center marks. Stitch in place, using ¼"-wide seam allowance.

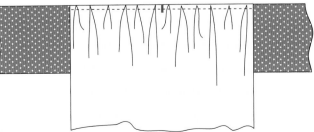

10. Fold waistband in half lengthwise, right sides together. Starting at apron's edge, stitch along bottom edge and side edge of waistband, leaving apron's gathered edge free of stitching. Repeat for other waistband side. Clip corners, turn right side out, and press.

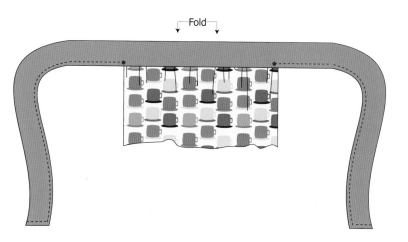

Fold

| Apron | FIRST CUT | |
	Number of Strips or Pieces	Dimensions
Fabric A Apron Skirt ½ yard	1	15" x 31"
Fabric B Apron Ruffle, Pocket Top Accent & Pocket Lining ⅔ yard	2 1 1	7½" x 42" 5½" x 8" 3" x 5½"
Fabric C Waistband & Pocket Bottom Accent ⅜ yard	2 1	4½" x 42" 1½" x 5½"
Fabric D Pocket Scrap	1	4½" x 5½"
1" Button - 1		

11. Press waistband's raw edge ¼" to wrong side, covering aprons gathered raw edge of apron. Topstitch waistband along all edges.

12. For Ruffle: Sew 7½" x 42" Fabric B strips together end-to-end to make one continuous Fabric B strip. Cut strip to measure 7½" x 60". On wrong side of fabric mark center.

13. Fold strip from step 12 in half lengthwise, right sides together, to measure 3¾" x 60". Stitch both short sides. Turn right side out and press.

14. Using a basting stitch, sew ⅛" and ¼" from raw edge of ruffle. Pin ruffle to apron at center marks. Gather ruffle evenly to match apron edge and stitch. Press ruffle with seam going toward apron. Top stitch along apron bottom edge to hold seam in place.

Napkins

Supplies
for two napkins

Napkin - ½ yard
 Two 14½" squares
 Backing - ½ yard
 Two 14½" squares

1. Layer one 14½" Napkin square and one Backing square right sides together. Using ¼"-wide seam, stitch around all edges, leaving a 4" opening on one side for turning. Clip corners, turn, and press. Hand-stitch opening closed. Make two.

2. Edge stitch around outside edge of each napkin.

Finished Size:
14" square

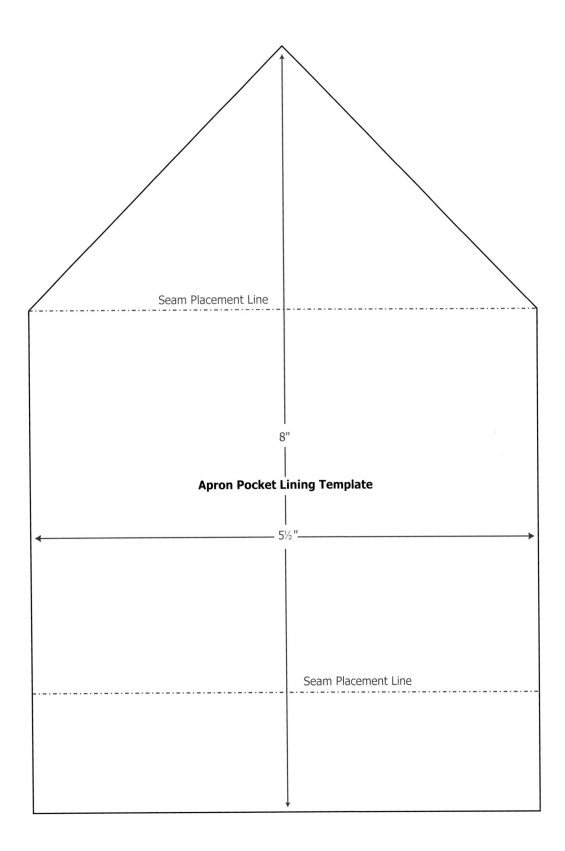

Seam Placement Line

8"

Apron Pocket Lining Template

5½"

Seam Placement Line

Placemats

Instructions are for two placemats.

Fabric Requirements and Cutting Instructions
Read all instructions before beginning and use ¼"-wide seam allowances throughout. Read Cutting Strips and Pieces on page 124 prior to cutting fabric.

Getting Started
Finish your kitchen ensemble by making an assortment of potholders, some with appliqués and some using theme fabrics.

Placemat Finished Size: 17" x 13"	FIRST CUT		SECOND CUT	
	Number of Strips or Pieces	Dimensions	Number of Pieces	Dimensions
Fabric A Center ⅓ yard	1	8½" x 42"	2	8½" x 9½"
Fabric B First Border ⅙ yard	1	3½" x 42"	2	3½" x 10½"
Fabric C Second Border ⅛ yard	1	2½" x 42"	2	2½" x 12½"
Fabric D Third Border ¼ yard	1	4½" x 42"	2	4½" x 10½"
Fabric E Fourth Border ⅛ yard	1	2½" x 42"	2	2½" x 13½"
Binding ⅜ yard	4	2¾" x 42"		
Backing - ⅔ yard Batting - Two 21" x 17"				

1. Note: A partial seam is used to sew the following pieces together. Start at mark (red dot) and stitch to outside edge in direction indicated with red arrow. Sew one 8½" x 9½" Fabric A piece to one 3½" x 10½" Fabric B piece as shown. Press. Make two.

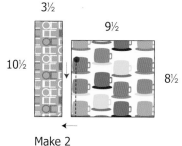

Make 2

- Sew a partial seam starting at mark and stitching to outside edge.

2. Sew one 2½" x 12½" Fabric C piece to one unit from step 1 as shown. Press. Make two.

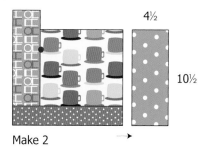

Make 2

3. Sew one 4½" x 10½" Fabric D piece to one unit from step 2 as shown. Press. Make two.

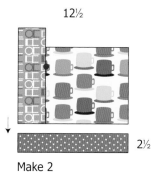

Make 2

4. Sew one 2½" x 13½" Fabric E piece to one unit from step 3 as shown. Press. Make two.

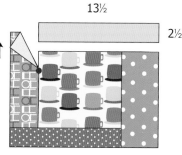

Make 2

5. Finish stitching the block together starting at mark and sewing to outside edge. Press. Make two. Block measures 12½" x 16½".

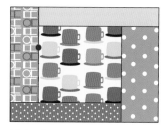

Make 2

Layering and Finishing

1. Referring to Layering the Quilt on page 126, arrange and baste backing, batting, and top together. Hand or machine quilt as desired.

2. Refer to Binding the Quilt on page 126. Use 2¾"-wide binding strips to bind quilt.

Potholders

Fabric Requirements and Cutting Instructions

Read all instructions before beginning and use ¼"-wide seam allowances throughout. Read Cutting Strips and Pieces on page 124 prior to cutting fabric.

Getting Started
Finish your kitchen ensemble by making an assortment of potholders, some with appliqués and some using theme fabrics.

Adding the Appliqués

Refer to appliqué instructions on page 125 if adding an appliqué to center panel. Our instructions are for Quick-Fuse Appliqué, but if you prefer hand appliqué, reverse patterns and add ¼"-wide seam allowances.

1. Use pattern to trace coffee cup and steam on paper side of fusible web. Use appropriate fabrics to prepare all appliqués for fusing.

2. Refer to photo on page 72 to position and fuse appliqués to 6½" x 7½" Fabric A piece. Finish appliqué edges with machine satin stitch or other decorative stitching as desired.

Making the Potholder

1. Sew one 6½" x 7½" Fabric A piece or appliqué unit between two 1" x 6½" Fabric B pieces. Press seams toward Fabric B.

2. Sew unit from step 1 between two 1" x 8½" Fabric B piece. Press seams toward Fabric B.

Layering and Finishing

1. Referring to Layering the Quilt on page 126, arrange and baste backing, batting, and top together. Hand or machine quilt as desired.

2. Refer to Binding the Quilt on page 126. Use 2¾"-wide binding strip to bind quilt.

Kitchen Cuties Potholder
Pattern is reversed for use
with Quick-Fuse Appliqué (page 125)

Tracing Line —————————
Tracing Line - - - - - - - - - - - - - - -
(will be hidden behind other fabrics)

Potholder Finished Size: 8" x 9" For one potholder	FIRST CUT	
	Number of Strips or Pieces	Dimensions
Fabric A Center Scrap	1	6½" x 7½"
Fabric B Border ⅛ yard	2 2	1" x 8½" 1" x 6½"
Binding ⅛ yard	1	2¾" x 42"

Appliqué - Assorted scraps
Backing - Fat Quarter
Heat Resistant Batting (Insul-Bright) 12" x 13"
Lightweight Fusible Web (18"-wide) Scrap
Stabilizer (20"-wide) Scrap

Kitschy Kitchen
Decor

1 DAY

KITSCHY WALL ART

If you love a kitschy kitchen you may not be able to part with this sweet and trendy trio of fabric wall art. The assembly of the stretcher bars, wrapping the fabric and appliquéing your designs will take approximately 3 hours. That's only about an hour each. What I always end up fussing over the most is making my fabric choices. Always allow plenty of time to do this – this is your creativity at work!

TRENDY TOWELS

Now my recommendation for these is Decorative Use Only! Find some coordinating terry towels to actually wipe your hands while you admire your handy work on these. Again the really fun part is picking your color story and collecting the right fabrics to bring your designs to life. The actual assembly will be around 3½ hours. Show these off every chance you get!

How long it will take you to accomplish tasks is an estimate and may vary greatly per individual. You may want to allow extra time for any distractions that may come up – like hunting down your seam ripper. (Happens to the best of us!)

Supplies
. . . .

Background - ½ yard
    Three 15" x 13"
Appliqués - Assorted Scraps
Rickrack Trim - 1½ yards
Brown Trim - ½ yard
Heavyweight Fusible Web (18"-wide)
    1 yard
Stretched Canvas Boards - (3) 8" x 10"
Fabric Glue
Staple Gun & Staples
Picture or Sawtooth Hangers

Wall Art

Getting Started
Decorate your kitchen with these no-sew art panels.

Making the Wall Art
We used stretched canvas boards. If using stretcher bars to make frame, cover frame with heavyweight fabric to stabilize frame before continuing.

1. Pull 13" x 15" Background piece around frame, staple in the middle on each side, pulling fabric tightly to obtain good tension. Continue process, working from center, stretching and stapling fabric, stopping at corners.

Back View

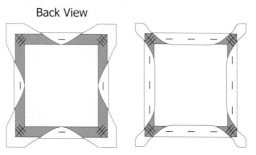

2. Pull corner tight and check front to make sure fabric is taut. Fold excess fabric at 90°, crease, and form corner. Staple tightly to back.

Adding the Appliqués

Refer to appliqué instructions on page 125. Our project is an art piece requiring no laundering. We used heavyweight fusible web since appliqué edges will not have a finished stitch treatment to edges.

1. Use patterns on pages 80, 81, 82, and 83 to trace large, medium, and small mushrooms and flowers, three small leaves, and large owl on paper side of heavyweight fusible web. Use appropriate fabrics to prepare all appliqués for fusing.

2. Refer to photo on page 78 to position and glue trim to background piece as desired.

3. Refer to photo on page 78 to position and fuse appliqués to background piece centering designs. Note: Place folded fabric or towel under center of canvas frame to make foundation for fusing.

4. Attach sawtooth hanger or wire picture hanger to back of each wall piece. Add any additional embellishments as desired.

Medium Flower

Small Flower

Large Flower

Patterns are reversed for use
with Quick-Fuse Appliqué (page 125)

Tracing Line _____
Tracing Line - - - - - - - - - - - - - - - - - - -
(will be hidden behind other fabrics)

Make 3

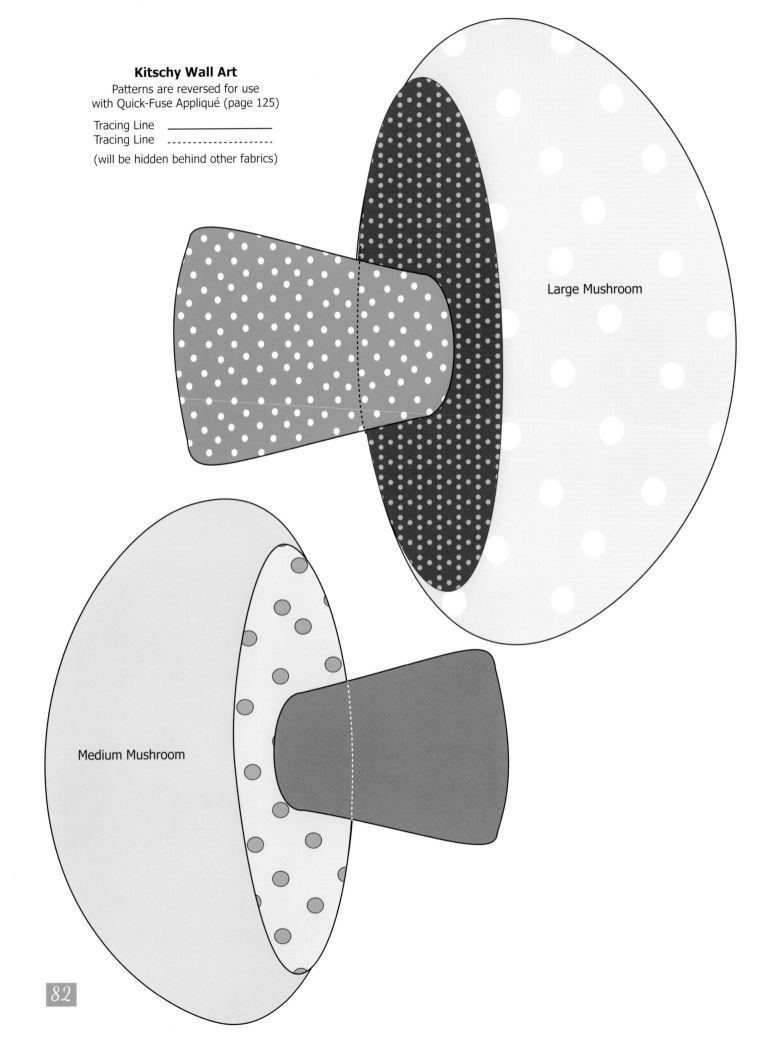

Kitschy Wall Art

Patterns are reversed for use
with Quick-Fuse Appliqué (page 125)

Tracing Line _____

Tracing Line - - - - - - - - - - - - - - - -

(will be hidden behind other fabrics)

Large Mushroom

Medium Mushroom

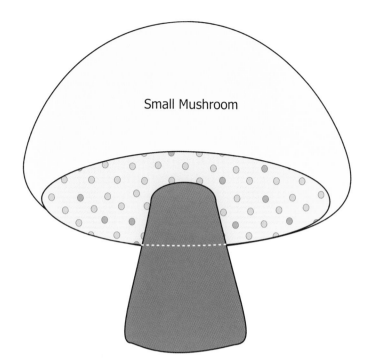

Small Mushroom

Decorative Kitchen Towels

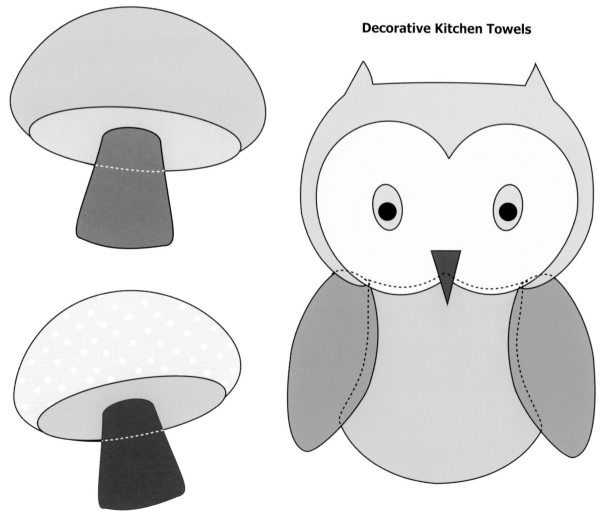

Towels

Fabric Requirements and Cutting Instructions

Read all instructions before beginning and use ¼"-wide seam allowances throughout. Read Cutting Strips and Pieces on page 124 prior to cutting fabric.

Getting Started
These towels are a little bit retro with a modern twist to rock your kitchen.

Making the Towel

Instructions are for one towel but two different versions are shown below chart. Make as many as desired following same instructions and changing the fabrics and appliqués.

1. Refer to photo on page 78 and layout for all step instructions. Sew one 5½" x 21¾" Fabric A piece to one 1¼" x 5½" Fabric B piece. Press toward Fabric B.

2. Sew trim to unit from step 1 approximately 1" from Fabric B inside edge.

3. Fold one 1½" x 22½" Fabric C strip in half lengthwise wrong sides together to make one ¾" x 22½" folded piece. Press. Matching raw edges, layer folded strip on one 4½" x 22½" Fabric D strip. Baste in place. Make two.

4. Sew unit from step 1 between two units from step 3. Press.

Adding the Appliqués

Refer to appliqué instructions on page 125. Our instructions are for Quick-Fuse Appliqué, but if you prefer hand appliqué, reverse patterns and add ¼"-wide seam allowances.

1. Use patterns on pages 83 to trace owl or mushrooms on paper side of fusible web. Use appropriate fabrics to prepare all appliqués for fusing.

2. Referring to photo on page 78 and layout to position and fuse appliqués to towel. Finish appliqué edges with machine satin stitch or other decorative stitching as desired.

Kitchen Towel Finished Size: 13" x 22"	FIRST CUT	
	Number of Strips or Pieces	Dimensions
Fabric A Center Panel ¼ yard	1	5½" x 21¾"
Fabric B Bottom Accent Scrap	1	1¼" x 5½"
Fabric C Side Accent ⅙ yard	2	1½" x 22½"
Fabric D Side Accent Border ⅓ yard	2	4½" x 22½"
Backing ½ yard	1	13½" x 22½"

Appliqués - Assorted scraps
Lightweight Fusible Web (18"-wide)
  ¼ yard
Stabilizer (20"-wide)
  ¼ yard
Rickrack Trim - ⅜ yard
Rickrack Trim - ¼ yard

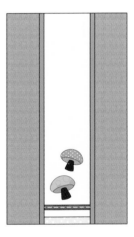

Finishing the Towels

Layer and center towel top and backing right sides together. Using ¼"-wide seam, stitch around all edges, leaving a 4" opening on one side for turning. Clip corners, turn, and press. Hand-stitch opening closed.

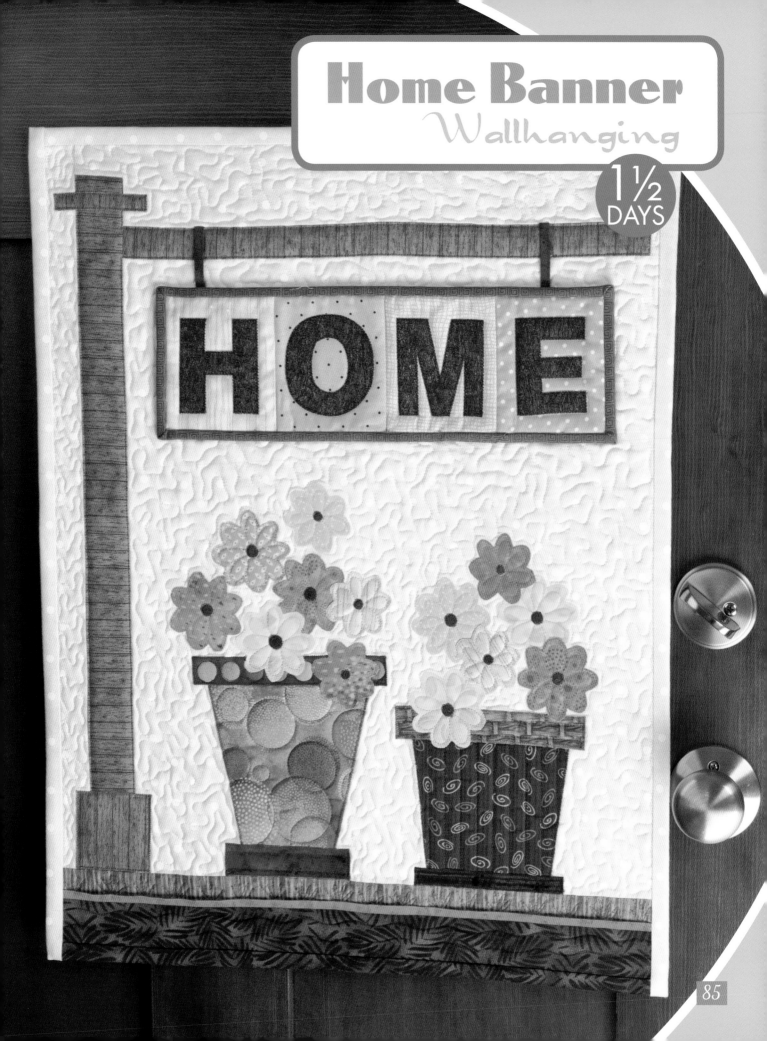

Home Banner
Wallhanging

1½ DAYS

Weekend Planner

● ● ● ● ● ● ● ● ● ● ● ● ●

This project combines both piecing and appliqué. Even though there are lots of little parts and pieces, because it is small, it can still be quick to accomplish.

FRIDAY EVENING

This one I was able to do completely from my scrap bin. Your first step should be to check out what you have on hand before you make plans to visit the fabric store. Tape small scraps of your choices to a piece of paper and bring it to your quilt shop so you can coordinate your purchases with what you already have. Double check that you have the appliqué thread colors and fusible web before you head to the store.

SATURDAY MORNING

It's fantastic to have all of your materials in house ready to go so you can get started first thing in the morning. Cutting all your strips and pieces for the background can be done in about 30 minutes. Trace your designs and cut out your appliqué shapes in an hour. Time to get a second cup of coffee and a banana muffin to keep you company while you move to your next steps. (Everyone can reach for their own muffin this morning — you're not cooking breakfast today!)

Piecing the background of the banner and the HOME sign may take about an hour to put together. Then the real fun starts when you lay out the appliqué pieces. You can follow my layout, or experiment with different place-ments of the flowers. Fuse them all in place and give yourself a lunch break.

SUNDAY AFTERNOON

Set your machine for zigzag and appliqué everything in place. You can possibly knock this out in around 2½ hours. Keeping your focus is important to productivity and you'll achieve that sense of accomplishment. Allow a good hour to quilt and bind the little "HOME" sign. You're done for now. Before you attach the HOME sign, send the banner out to your favorite machine quilter — or this one is small enough to do on your home machine, if you prefer.

How long it will take you to accomplish tasks is an estimate and may vary greatly per individual. You may want to allow extra time for any distractions that may come up – like hunting down your seam ripper. (Happens to the best of us!)

Home Banner Wallhanging Finished Size: 20½" x 26" Home: 14½" x 4½"	FIRST CUT		SECOND CUT	
	Number of Strips or Pieces	Dimensions	Number of Pieces	Dimensions
Fabric A Background ⅝ yard	1	17½" x 42"	1	17½" x 19½"
			1	3" x 17½"
	1	1½" x 42"	1	1½" x 23"
			1	1½" x 2"
			1	1½" x 1"
Fabric B Post ⅛ yard	1	2" x 42"	1	2" x 22"
			1	1½" x 17"
Fabric C Grass ⅛ yard	1	1½" x 42"	1	1½" x 20"
Fabric D Mock Piping ⅛ yard	1	1" x 42"	1	1" x 20"
Fabric E Bottom Accent ⅛ yard	1	2" x 42"	1	2" x 20"
Fabric F HOME Background scrap each of 4 Fabrics	1*	4" x 4½" *cut for each fabric		
HOME Banner Hangers Scrap	1	1" x 6"		
Quilt Binding (Top & Sides) ⅓ yard	3	2¾" x 42"		
Quilt Binding (Bottom) ⅛ yard	1	2¾" x 42"		
HOME Banner Binding ⅛ yard	1	1¾" x 42" ¼" finished binding		

Appliqués - Assorted scraps
Quilt Backing - ¾ yard
HOME Backing - Fat Quarter
Batting - 24" x 30" & 18" x 8"
Lightweight Fusible Web (18"-wide) - ½ yard
Stabilizer (20"-wide) - ¾ yard

Fabric Requirements and Cutting Instructions

Read all instructions before beginning and use ¼"-wide seam allowances throughout. Read Cutting Strips and Pieces on page 124 prior to cutting fabric.

Getting Started

The separate HOME banner is attached with tabs on the post above the colorful flowerpots. Refer to Accurate Seam Allowance on page 124. Whenever possible use Assembly Line Method on page 124. Press seams in direction of arrows.

Making the Quilt

1. Sew one 1½" x 17" Fabric B strip to one 1½" x 1" Fabric A piece as shown. Press.

2. Sew unit from step 1 between one 3" x 17½" Fabric A strip and one 17½" x 19½" Fabric A piece as shown. Press.

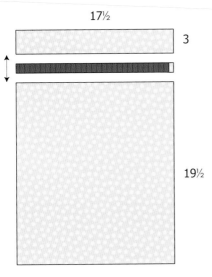

3. Sew one 2" x 22" Fabric B strip to one 1½" x 2" Fabric A piece as shown. Press. Sew this unit to one 1½" x 23" Fabric A strip. Press.

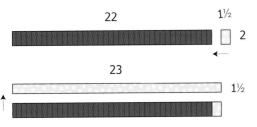

Home Banner Wallhanging
20½" x 26"

4. Fold one 1" x 20" Fabric D strip in half lengthwise wrong sides together to make one ½" x 20" folded piece. Press. Matching raw edges, layer folded strip on one 2" x 20" Fabric E strip. Baste in place. Sew one 1½" x 20" Fabric C strip to unit from this step as shown. Press.

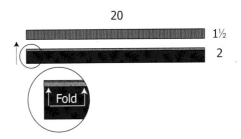

5. Sew unit from step 3 to unit from step 2 as shown. Press. Sew this unit to unit from step 4. Press.

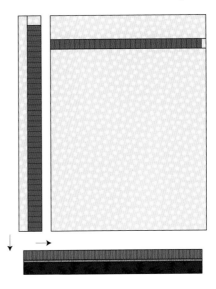

6. For HOME banner arrange and sew together four different 4" x 4½" Fabric F pieces as shown. Press.

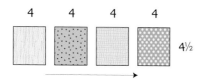

Adding the Appliqués
Refer to appliqué instructions on page 125. Our instructions are for Quick-Fuse Appliqué, but if you prefer hand appliqué, reverse patterns and add ¼"-wide seam allowances.

1. Use patterns on pages 88, 89, and 90 to trace large and small flowerpots, post base, post top accent, eight large flowers, and five small flowers on paper side of fusible web. Use appropriate fabrics to prepare all appliqués for fusing.

2. Refer to photo on page 85 and layout on page 87 to position and fuse appliqués to quilt. Finish appliqué edges with machine satin stitch or other decorative stitching as desired.

3. Repeat steps 1 and 2 to trace HOME on paper side of fusible web. Fuse to appropriate fabrics, and fuse to HOME pieced background unit.

Layering and Finishing

1. Fold one 1" x 6" Home Banner Hanger in half lengthwise and press. Open and fold raw edges to center pressed line. Press. Fold again in half lengthwise. Press. Top stitch folds in place. Cut crosswise in half to make two ¼" x 3" pieces.

2. Referring to photo on page 85, layout on page 87 and diagram below, determine hanger placement on post and mark. Unstitch along top edge seam line of post at placement marks. Insert one hanger end into seam ¼" and stitch in place. Repeat for other hanger.

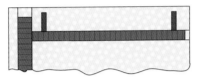

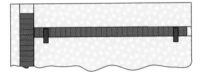

3. Referring to Layering the Quilt on page 126, arrange and baste backing, batting, and quilt top together. Hand or machine quilt as desired, keeping tabs free of stitching.

4. Refer to Binding the Quilt on page 126. Sew 2¾"-wide binding strips to top and bottom of quilt using two different fabrics. Sew binding strips to sides. Bind quilt to finish.

5. Repeat step 3 to arrange, baste and quilt HOME banner.

6. Refer to Binding the Quilt on page 126. Use 1¾"-wide binding strips to bind HOME banner. Attach hanging tabs to back of banner along top edge. Banner binding finishes a narrow ¼".

Home Banner Wallhanging
Patterns are reversed for use
with Quick-Fuse Appliqué (page 125)

Tracing Line   ——————————
Tracing Line   - - - - - - - - - - - - - - - -
(will be hidden behind other fabrics)

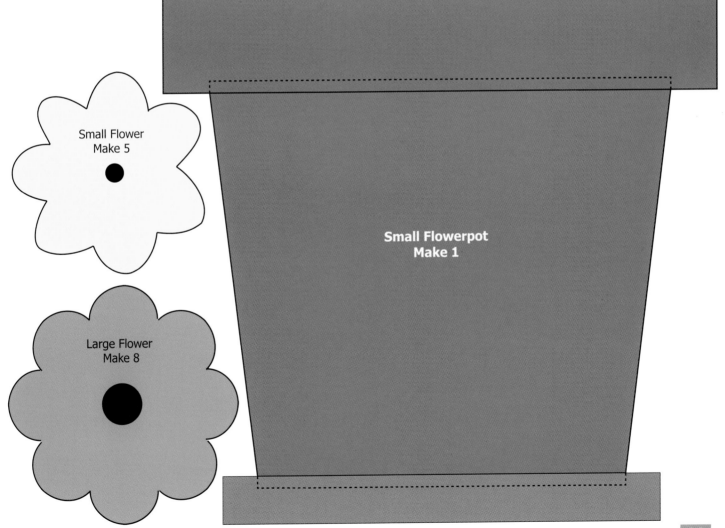

Small Flower
Make 5

Large Flower
Make 8

Small Flowerpot
Make 1

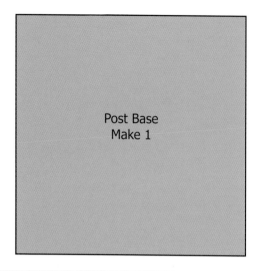

Post Base
Make 1

Home Banner Wallhanging
Patterns are reversed for use
with Quick-Fuse Appliqué (page 125)

Tracing Line _____
Tracing Line - - - - - - - - - - - - - - - - -
(will be hidden behind other fabrics)

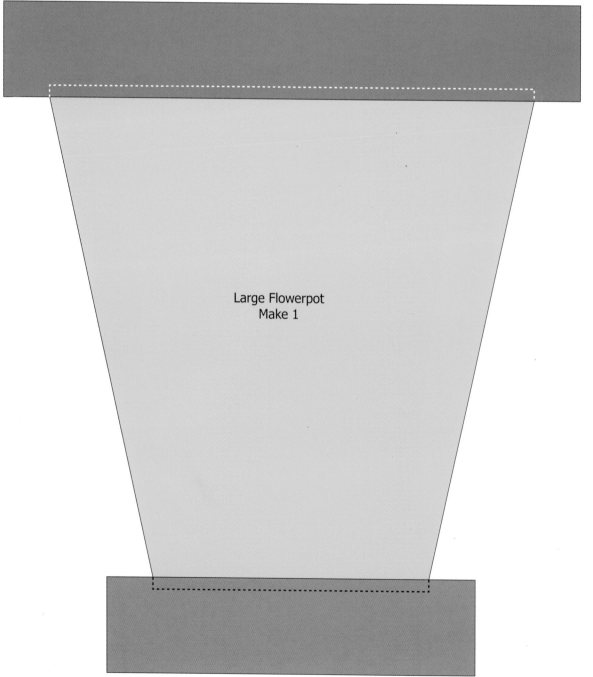

Post Top Accent
Make 1

Large Flowerpot
Make 1

Log Cabin Path

Throw Quilt

1½ DAYS

Weekend Planner

Log Cabin designs are perennial classics; however, it's always fun to take the design down a new path. One of the elements that makes this layout unique is the amount of open, light space that is highlighted with quilting. The continuous feather quilting design really creates movement throughout the quilt. My machine quilter gets big kudos for this!

FRIDAY EVENING

It's a good idea to get your fabrics selected and your plan put together before sewing day. It just makes you feel so organized. Sometimes you can start by choosing your border fabric first and then coordinate the block fabrics to go with that. The corner squares will create a strong visual chain pattern if they have good contrast to the background fabric.

SATURDAY MORNING AND AFTERNOON

Isn't it a fabulous feeling when you wake up in the morning and realize that it's a sewing day! Cutting strips is usually pretty fast – it will likely take you an hour to complete the cutting. You'll be looking at a good 3 plus hours of focused piecing to complete the blocks. It's usually helpful to set goals. I would suggest a goal of completing the log cabin part of the blocks by lunch. Take a nice break and then finish them up in the afternoon.

SUNDAY MORNING

While sipping on your morning coffee, start your day by admiring your wonderful handiwork from yesterday. Choose the layout you want and join the blocks together over the next hour and a half. With one more hour you can get your borders added. Quilt top complete!

How long it will take you to accomplish tasks is an estimate and may vary greatly per individual. You may want to allow extra time for any distractions that may come up – like hunting down your seam ripper. *(Happens to the best of us!)*

Log Cabin Path Throw Quilt Finished Size: 44" x 53"	FIRST CUT		SECOND CUT	
	Number of Strips or Pieces	Dimensions	Number of Pieces	Dimensions
Fabric A Background 1⅓ yards	14 4	2½" x 42" 1½" x 42"	40 40	2½" x 7½" 2½" x 5½"
Fabric B Block Large & Small Squares ⅜ yard	2 4	2½" x 42" 1½" x 42"	20	2½" squares
Fabric C Block 1 First Accent ⅙ yard	2	1½" x 42"	10 10	1½" x 3½" 1½" x 2½"
Fabric D Block 2 First Accent ⅙ yard	2	1½" x 42"	10 10	1½" x 3½" 1½" x 2½"
Fabric E Block 1 Third Accent & Block 2 Second Accent ⅓ yard	5	1½" x 42"	10 20 10	1½" x 5½" 1½" x 4½" 1½" x 3½"
Fabric F Block 1 Second Accent ¼ yard	3	1½" x 42"	10 10	1½" x 4½" 1½" x 3½"
Fabric G Block 2 Third Accent ¼ yard	3	1½" x 42"	10 10	1½" x 5½" 1½" x 4½"
First Border ¼ yard	5	1" x 42"	2	1" x 36½"
Second Border ¼ yard	5	1" x 42"	2	1" x 37½"
Outside Border ½ yard	5	3" x 42"	2	3" x 38½"
Binding ½ yard	5	2¾" x 42"		
Backing - 2⅞ yards Batting - 50" x 59"				

Fabric Requirements and Cutting Instructions Read all instructions before beginning and use ¼"-wide seam allowances throughout. Read Cutting Strips and Pieces on page 124 prior to cutting fabric.

Getting Started This stylish geometric quilt uses a traditional block design set with a contemporary flair. Blocks are made using two different fabric combinations. Block measures 9½" square (unfinished). Refer to Accurate Seam Allowance on page 124. Whenever possible use Assembly Line Method on page 124. Press seams in direction of arrows.

Assembling the Quilt

1. Sew one 2½" Fabric B square to one 1½" x 2½" Fabric C piece as shown. Press. Sew this unit to one 1½" x 3½" Fabric C piece. Press. Make ten.

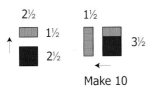

Make 10

2. Sew one unit from step 1 to one 1½" x 3½" Fabric F piece as shown. Press. Sew this unit to one 1½" x 4½" Fabric F piece. Press. Make ten.

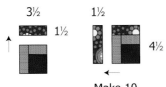

Make 10

3. Sew one unit from step 2 to one 1½" x 4½" Fabric E piece as shown. Press. Sew this unit to one 1½" x 5½" Fabric E piece. Press. Make ten.

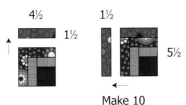

Make 10

4. Sew one unit from step 3 between two 2½" x 5½" Fabric A piece as shown. Press. Make ten.

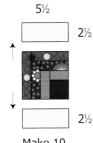

Make 10

5. Sew together lengthwise one 1½" x 42" Fabric A strip and one 1½" x 42" Fabric B strip to make a strip set. Press seams toward Fabric B. Make four. Cut strip sets into eighty 1½"-wide segments as shown.

Make 4
Cut 80 segments

Log Cabin Path *Throw Quilt*

44" x 53"

6. Sew two units from step 5 together as shown. Refer to Twisting Seams on page 124. Press. Make forty.

Make 40

7. Sew one unit from step 6 to one 2½" x 7½" Fabric A piece as shown. Press. Make forty.

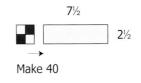

Make 40

8. Sew one unit from step 4 between two units from step 7 as shown. Press. Make ten and label Block 1. Block measures 9½" square.

Block 1

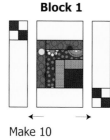

Make 10
Block measures 9½"

9. Referring to steps 1-8, sew ten of Block 2. Block 2 uses the following fabrics; 2½" Fabric B squares, 1½" x 2½" and 1½" x 3½" Fabric D pieces, 1½" x 3½" and 1½" x 4½" Fabric E pieces, 1½" x 4½" and 1½" x 5½" Fabric G pieces, 2½" x 5½" Fabric A pieces, and units from step 7. Press seams as indicated in step diagrams until step 8. Note: Press seams pressed in opposite direction from Block 1 as shown below.

Block 2

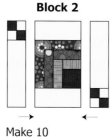

Make 10
Block measures 9½"

10. Arrange and sew together two of Block 1 and two of Block 2 as shown. Press. Make three and label these rows 1, 3, and 5.

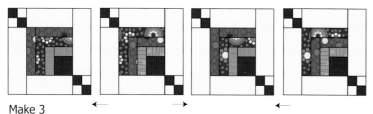

Make 3
Rows 1, 3 & 5

11. Arrange and sew together two of Block 2 and two of Block 1 as shown. Press. Make two and label these rows 2 and 4.

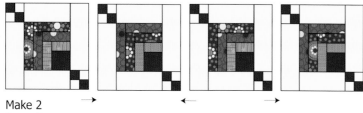

Make 2
Rows 2 & 4

12. Referring to layout on page 93, arrange and sew together rows 1-5. Press.

Adding the Borders

1. Sew two 1" x 36½" First Border strips to top and bottom of quilt. Press seams toward border.

2. Refer to Adding the Borders on page 126. Sew 1" x 42" First Border strips together end-to-end to make one continuous 1"-wide First Border strip. Measure quilt through center from top to bottom including borders just added. Cut two 1"-wide First Border strips to this measurement. Sew to sides of quilt. Press.

3. Sew two 1" x 37½" Second Border strips to top and bottom of quilt. Press seams toward border just sewn. Refer to step 2 to join, measure, trim, and sew 1"-wide Second Border strips to sides of quilt. Press.

4. Sew two 3" x 38½" Outside Border strips to top and bottom of quilt. Press seams toward border just sewn. Refer to step 2 to join, measure, trim, and sew 3"-wide Outside Border strips to sides of quilt. Press.

Layering and Finishing

1. Cut backing crosswise into two equal pieces. Sew pieces together lengthwise to make one 50" x 80" (approximate) backing piece. Press and trim to 50" x 59".

2. Referring to Layering the Quilt on page 126, arrange and baste backing, batting, and top together. Hand or machine quilt as desired.

3. Refer to Binding the Quilt on page 126. Sew 2¾" x 42" binding strips end-to-end to make one continuous 2¾"-wide binding strip. Bind quilt to finish.

Re-Usable Weekend Bags
Lunch and Shopping

1 DAY

Weekend Planner

These bags are sturdy and packed with personality (and lunch!). Since you will be using these over and over, don't shy away from the few hours it takes to construct each one. This project uses simple construction and is not complicated. However, the extra time that it takes to do the machine quilting and the seams along the gussets is what gives them structure and helps them maintain their shape. (Not to mention you want them to survive several spins through the laundry.) Allow yourself a good 4 hours per bag.

Re-Usable Weekend Bags Finished Size: 12" x 13" x 4" 9" x 10" x 4"	FIRST CUT		SECOND CUT	
	Number of Strips or Pieces	Dimensions	Number of Pieces	Dimensions
Shopping Bag				
Fabric A Top Section ⅓ yard	1	9½" x 42"	2	9½" x 16½"
Fabric B Bottom Section ¼ yard	1	6½" x 42"	2	6½" x 16½"
Fabric C Handles ½ yard	2	6" x 42"		
Lining ½ yard	1	15½" x 42"	2	15½" x 16½"
Backing - ½ yard (will not show) Batting - Two 17" x 17½" and two 1½" x 42"				
Lunch Bag				
Fabric A Top Section ⅓ yard	1	7½" x 42"	2	7½" x 13½"
Fabric B Bottom Section ¼ yard	1	5½" x 42"	2	5½" x 13½"
Fabric C Handles ½ yard	2	4½" x 42"		
Lining ½ yard	1	12½" x 42"	2	12½" x 13½"
Backing - ½ yard Batting - Two 14" x 14½" and two 1" x 42"				

Fabric Requirements and Cutting Instructions

Read all instructions before beginning and use ¼"-wide seam allowances throughout. Read Cutting Strips and Pieces on page 124 prior to cutting fabric. Both bags are made using the same techniques, only the fabric cuts vary from bag to bag.

Getting Started

Going green has never been easier. Just whip up these simple-to-construct bags to take on your shopping sprees. These bags are also great gifts for family and friends.

Making the Shopping Bag

1. For shopping bag, press 6" x 42" Fabric C strip in half lengthwise wrong sides together. Unfold strip and bring outside long edges in to centerline (wrong sides together). Press. Fold again and press to make a 1½"-wide folded strip.

2. Unfold strip from step 1. Lay two 1½" x 42" Batting strips on side of centerfold line. Fold outside edges to center covering batting and fold again. Press. Stitch ⅛" and ½" from both sides of outside edges. Make two. Trim handles to measure 36".

3. Place one 36"-long handle on one marked 9½" x 16½" Fabric A piece 4½" from outside edges as shown. Pin in place. Sew this unit to one marked 6½" x 16½" Fabric B piece as shown. Press. Make two.

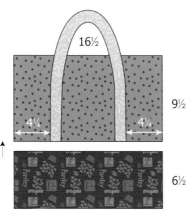

4. Referring to Layering the Quilt on page 126, arrange and baste backing, batting, and units from step 4 or 5 together. Hand or machine quilt as desired. Keep handles free of quilting. Trim backing and batting to match unit edges.

5. Stitch handle in place along previous handle stitch lines stopping stitching approximately ¾" – 1" from top edge.

6. Place quilted units from step 5 right sides together matching Fabric B seam line. Sew along sides and bottom edge leaving top edge free of stitches.

7. Fold one bottom corner of unit from step 8, matching side seam to bottom seam. Draw a 4" line 2" from bottom corner as shown. Sew on drawn line, anchoring stitches. Fold stitched corner to bottom seam and tack in place for stability. Repeat for other side.

8. Repeat steps 6 and 7 to stitch lining pieces, right sides together, leaving a 5" opening on one side for turning and top edge free of stitches.

9. Turn bag right side out. Place bag into lining piece right sides together matching raw edges and seam lines. Using ¼"-wide seam allowance, sew along top edge. Turn bag through lining opening and hand stitch opening closed.

10. Refer to photo on page 95 to create a mock binding. Stitch-in-the-ditch along top seam line of bag and lining. Secure handles by stitching across width close to mock binding.

11. For side and bottom gussets, refer to photo to stitch ⅛" along each side edge through all thicknesses (from top edge to bottom corner formed in step 9). Repeat for all sides. Repeat for front and back bottom edges.

Making the Lunch Bag

1. Use 4½" x 42" Fabric C strip and referring to steps 1 and 2, make two 1"-wide (approximate) handles. Trim to 30". Top stitch ⅛" from both outside edges and down center.

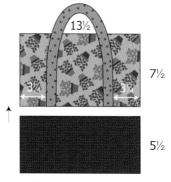

Make 2

2. Place one 30"-long handle on one marked 7½" x 13½" Fabric A piece 3¼" from outside edges as shown. Pin in place. Sew this unit to one marked 5½" x 13½" Fabric B piece as shown. Press. Make two.

3. Follow steps 4-11 for Shopping Bag. Use 12½" x 13½" lining pieces in step 8 and leave 13½" top edge free of stiches.

All Nighter
Lap Quilt

1 DAY

Weekend Planner

Remember when you could actually pull an all-nighter? Maybe this will just be a late-nighter.

SATURDAY MORNING

Feel free to sleep in a little so you can stay up late tonight. After you get yourself going, head on out to the fabric store to select your fabrics. You'll need eight greens, eight blues, five browns and ten tans. You may find several from your stash that will work too.

SATURDAY AFTERNOON

Relax and spend time in another fun activity. Just don't wear yourself out - you've got a late night ahead.

SATURDAY EVENING

Finish up dinner and make yourself a big cup of black tea with milk and sugar for energy. Cutting your pieces for this project may take a good hour or longer. Stack your fabrics by color so they are organized and ready to start your piecing. Line them up next to the machine and get that machine humming. Keep your focus and piecing these simple blocks shouldn't take more than a couple hours.

After piecing is complete, allow plenty of time to layout and organize the order that you want your blocks in. Don't fret, this may take you around 45 minutes. Once you've got a plan, lay out your blocks in order and keep rechecking as you're sewing to make sure you haven't lost track of your preferred arrangement. Don't worry, with a quilt design like this one, even if you do lose track, you may never be able to tell the difference. As long as all goes smoothly, piecing your top may only take around an hour or two. Hit the sack and don't make any early morning plans for the next day!

How long it will take you to accomplish tasks is an estimate and may vary greatly per individual. You may want to allow extra time for any distractions that may come up - like hunting down your seam ripper. *(Happens to the best of us!)*

All Nighter Lap Quilt Finished Size: 45" x 56"	FIRST CUT		SECOND CUT	
	Number of Strips or Pieces	Dimensions	Number of Pieces	Dimensions
Fabric A Block Centers scrap each of 10 Fabrics 	2*	3½" squares *cut for each fabric		
Fabric B Block Sashing ¼ yard each of 5 Fabrics 	4*	1½" x 42" *cut for each fabric	16*	1½" x 7½"
Fabric C Block Accents ⅙ yard each of 8 Fabrics 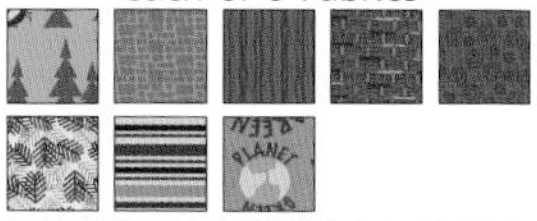	1*	3½" x 42" *cut for each fabric	5*	3½" x 7½"
Fabric D Block Accents ⅙ yard each of 8 Fabrics 	1*	3½" x 42" *cut for each fabric	5*	3½" x 7½"
 **Binding** ⅝ yard	6	2¾" x 42"		
Backing - 2⅞ yards Batting - 51" x 62"				

Fabric Requirements and Cutting Instructions Read all instructions before beginning and use ¼"-wide seam allowances throughout. Read Cutting Strips and Pieces on page 124 prior to cutting fabric.

Getting Started
Select two of your favorite colors to showcase in this scrappy quilt. Block measures 11½" square (unfinished). Refer to Accurate Seam Allowance on page 124. Whenever possible use Assembly Line Method on page 124. Press seams in direction of arrows.

Tip: Scrappy Quilts
Making a scrappy quilt can be time consuming, so here are some tips to speed up the process. This quilt uses ten assorted fabrics for the centers, five assorted fabrics for the block sashing, and eight assorted fabrics for each of the block accents. Each block consists of one sashing fabric (four matching 1½" x 7½" pieces), one center, and four assorted accent pieces. A trick is to place all of Fabric C pieces in one sack and all of the Fabric D pieces in another sack. When it is time to stitch one of these pieces, just grab one and sew. If the fabric selected was previously used in the current block, place it back in the sack and select another one.

This same technique can be used when laying out the quilt by just randomly selecting blocks and sewing them together into rows, making sure that no two alike fabrics are touching. If a planned out approach is desired, first determine how much time to devote to this process. After the time has expired, stop and sew rows together.

Making the Quilt

1. Sew one 1½" x 7½" Fabric B piece to one 3½" x 7½" Fabric D piece as shown. Press. Make two using matching Fabric B pieces and different Fabric D pieces.

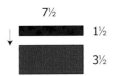

7½
1½
3½

Make 2
(in assorted Fabric D pieces)

2. Sew one 1½" x 7½" Fabric B piece (matching fabric used in step 1) to one 3½" x 7½" Fabric C piece as shown. Press. Make two using matching Fabric B pieces and different Fabric C pieces.

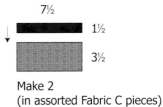

7½
1½
3½

Make 2
(in assorted Fabric C pieces)

3. A partial seam is used to sew the following pieces together. Start at mark (red dot) and stitch to outside edge in direction indicated with red arrow. Sew one 3½" Fabric A square to one unit from step 1. Press.

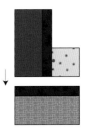

3½
3½

· Sew a partial seam starting at mark and stitching to outside edge.

4. Sew one unit from step 2 to unit from step 3 as shown. Press.

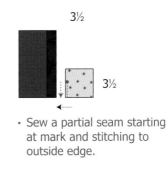

5. Sew remaining unit from step 1 to unit from step 4 as shown. Press.

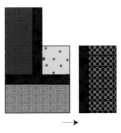

6. Sew remaining unit from step 2 to unit from step 5 as shown. Press.

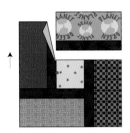

7. Finish stitching block together by starting at mark and sewing to outside edge. Press. Make twenty in assorted fabrics. Block measures 11½" square.

· Finish the block by sewing from mark to remaining outside edge.

Make 20
(in assorted Fabric C & D pieces)
Block measures 11½" square

Assembling the Quilt

1. Referring to layout, arrange and sew together five rows with four blocks each. Press seams in opposite direction from row to row.

2. Sew rows together and press.

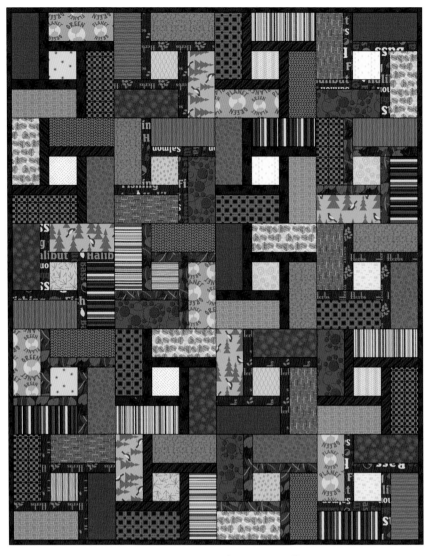

All Nighter Lap Quilt
45" x 56"

Layering and Finishing

1. Cut backing crosswise into two equal pieces. Sew pieces together lengthwise to make one 51" x 80" (approximate) backing piece. Press and trim to 51" x 62".

2. Referring to Layering the Quilt on page 126, arrange and baste backing, batting, and top together. Hand or machine quilt as desired.

3. Refer to Binding the Quilt on page 126. Sew 2¾" x 42" binding strips end-to-end to make one continuous 2¾"-wide binding strip. Bind quilt to finish.

Snowflake Winter
Coverlet

3½ DAYS

Weekend Planner

This is a bigger quilt that includes both piecing and appliqué, so we are going to spread the pre-sewing tasks over the week so you can hit the ground running this weekend.

WEDNESDAY EVENING

Flannels make the coziest winter quilts, so pop on over to the fabric store to select an assortment of flannels and cottons for this project. Yes, it's okay to combine both fabrics in one quilt. If any of your fabrics need pressing, take care of this tonight.

THURSDAY EVENING

Tonight trace your appliqué shapes onto fusible web and fuse to your selected snowflake fabric. You can even hand cut out the snowflake shapes in front of the TV.
(Max of three hours later – Snowflakes, done!)

FRIDAY EVENING

Tackle cutting the strips and pieces tonight and you will feel so accomplished. It will probably only take you about an hour and a half – so you will still have time to order pizza and watch a movie.

SATURDAY MORNING

Since you have a goal to complete – get yourself up bright and early. Anticipate about 3 to 4 hours to fuse and zigzag appliqué your snowflakes. Don't forget to stretch occasionally – you still have a full day of piecing ahead of you. Break for leftover pizza. Get on the floor and do some real stretches before you commence the next big leg of your project.

SATURDAY AFTERNOON

Load up several bobbins. Nothing's more annoying than to stop when you're on a roll to fill a bobbin. You'll want to allow 6 to 7 hours to piece the blocks for this one. You may be fatigued from all your appliquéing this morning. So you might think about setting the goal of getting half way through this afternoon and finish the rest tomorrow.

SUNDAY MORNING

After many days in a row of quilting, you will have to do your best to keep awake during this morning's sermon!

SUNDAY AFTERNOON

If you opted to finish the blocks today – naturally you'll need to do this first. For the final stretch of this project of laying out your blocks and piecing the top together, expect about 3 hours 'til you reach the finish line! Phew....that was quite an accomplishment. Call the quilter!

Snowflake Winter Coverlet Finished Size: 61" x 80½"	FIRST CUT		SECOND CUT	
	Number of Strips or Pieces	Dimensions	Number of Pieces	Dimensions
Fabric A Snowflake Background 1½ yards	4	12½" x 42"	12	12½" squares
Fabric B Unit 3 Center, Unit 6 Border & Sashing 1½ yards	2 19	3½" x 42" 2" x 42"	6 31 12 12	3½" x 9½" 2" x 18½" 2" x 6½" 2" x 3½"
Fabric C Unit 3 Border, Unit 4 Center, Unit 7 & 8 Borders 1⅛ yards Note: See yardage below for snowflake appliqués	2 6 5	3½" x 42" 2½" x 42" 2" x 42"	6 24 24 12 12	3½" x 9½" 2½" x 6½" 2½" squares 2" x 9½" 2" x 6½"
Fabric D Unit 4 & Unit 5 Borders ⅝ yard	8	2" x 42"	12 24 12	2" x 9½" 2" x 6½" 2" x 3½"
Fabric E Unit 5 Center ⅙ yard	1	3½" x 42"	6	3½" squares
Fabric F Unit 6 & Unit 7 Center ⅙ yard	1	3½" x 42"	6 6	3½" squares 2½" squares
Fabric G Unit 8 Center & Sashing Cornerstones ¼ yard	1 1	2½" x 42" 2" x 42"	6 20	2½" squares 2" squares
Fabric H Accent Square ½ yard	2	6½" x 42"	12	6½" squares
Binding ¾ yard	8	2¾" x 42"		

Snowflake Appliqués - 1½ yards
Backing - 5 yards
Batting - 69" x 88"
Lightweight Fusible Web (18"-wide) - 2⅔ yards
Stabilizer (20"-wide) - 2⅔ yards

Fabric Requirements and Cutting Instructions

Read all instructions before beginning and use ¼"-wide seam allowances throughout. Read Cutting Strips and Pieces on page 124 prior to cutting fabric.

Getting Started

This quilt, with its crisp clean lines and playful snowflakes, brings the fun of winter into your home. Block measures 18½" square (unfinished). Refer to Accurate Seam Allowance on page 124. Whenever possible use Assembly Line Method on page 124. Press seams in direction of arrows.

How long it will take you to accomplish tasks is an estimate and may vary greatly per individual. You may want to allow extra time for any distractions that may come up – like hunting down your seam ripper. *(Happens to the best of us!)*

Adding the Appliqués

Refer to appliqué instructions on page 125. Our instructions are for Quick-Fuse Appliqué, but if you prefer hand appliqué, add ¼"-wide seam allowances. Refer to page 107 for instructions to make complete large and medium snowflake patterns.

1. Use patterns on page 107 to trace six large snowflakes, six medium snowflakes, and twelve small snowflakes on paper side of fusible web. Use appropriate fabrics to prepare all appliqués for fusing.

2. Refer to photo on page 102 and diagram below to position and fuse large and medium snowflakes appliqués to 12½" Fabric A squares. Snowflake spokes are set so sections hang off the fabric as shown. Same size snowflakes are placed in the same position on fabric squares or arrange snowflakes and fuse as desired. Center small snowflakes on 6½" Fabric H squares and fuse in place. Finish appliqué edges with machine satin stitch or other decorative stitching as desired. Trim snowflake to match fabric squares. Make six large snowflakes and label Unit 1 and six medium snowflakes and label Unit 2.

6½

6½

12½

12½

Unit 1

12½

Make 6

12½

12½

Unit 2

Make 6

Making the Blocks

1. Sew one 3½" x 9½" Fabric B piece between two 2" x 9½" Fabric C pieces as shown. Press. Sew this unit between two 2" x 6½" Fabric C pieces as shown. Press. Make six and label Unit 3.

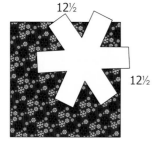

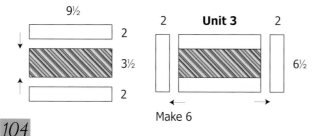

Make 6

2. Sew one Unit 1 to one Unit 3 as shown. Press. Make six and label Block 1A.

Block 1A

Make 6

3. Sew one 3½" x 9½" Fabric C piece between two 2" x 9½" Fabric D pieces as shown. Press. Sew this unit between two 2" x 6½" Fabric D pieces as shown. Press. Make six and label Unit 4.

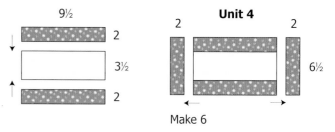

Make 6

4. Sew one Unit 2 to one Unit 4 as shown. Press. Make six and label Block 2A.

Block 2A

Make 6

5. Sew one 3½" Fabric E square between two 2" x 3½" Fabric D pieces as shown. Press. Sew this unit between two 2" x 6½" Fabric D pieces. Press. Make 6 and label Unit 5.

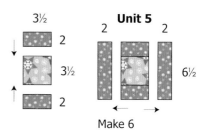

Make 6

6. Sew one 3½" Fabric F square between two 2" x 3½" Fabric B pieces as shown. Press. Sew this unit between two 2" x 6½" Fabric B pieces. Press. Make six and label Unit 6.

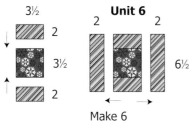

Unit 6

Make 6

7. Sew one 2½" Fabric F square between two 2½" Fabric C squares as shown. Press. Sew this unit between two 2½" x 6½" Fabric C pieces. Press. Make six and label Unit 7.

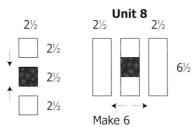

Unit 7

Make 6

8. Sew one 2½" Fabric G square between two 2½" Fabric C squares as shown. Press. Sew this unit between two 2½" x 6½" Fabric C pieces. Press. Make six and label Unit 8.

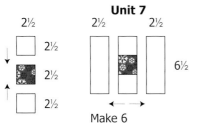

Unit 8

Make 6

9. Sew one Unit 7 between one Unit 5 and one small Snowlake unit as shown. Press. Make six and label Block 1B.

Block 1B

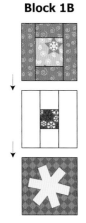

Make 6

Snowflake Winter *Coverlet*

61" x 80½"

10. Sew one Unit 6 between one Unit 8 and one small Snowlake unit as shown. Press. Make six and label Block 2B.

Block 2B

Make 6

11. Sew one Block 1A to one Block 1B together as shown. Press. Make six and relabel Block 1. Block measures 18½" square.

Block 1

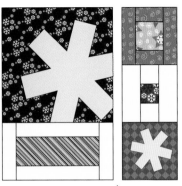

Make 6
Block measures 18½"

12. Sew one Block 2A to one Block 2B together as shown. Press. Make six and relabel Block 2. Block measures 18½" square.

Block 2

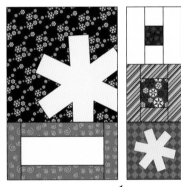

Make 6
Block measures 18½"

Assembling the Quilt

1. Arrange and sew together four 2" Fabric G squares to three 2" x 18½" Fabric B strips as shown. Press. Make five and label Rows 1, 3, 5, 7, and 9.

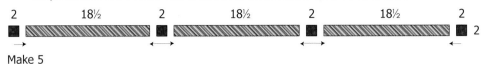

Make 5
Rows 1, 3, 5, 7 & 9

2. Arrange and sew together four 2" x 18½" Fabric B strips, two of Block 1, and one Block 2 as shown. Press. Make two and label Rows 2 and 6.

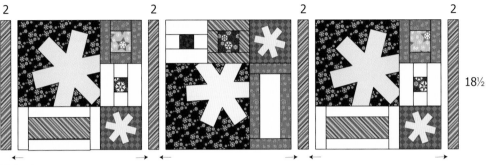

Make 2
Rows 2 & 6

3. Arrange and sew together four 2" x 18½" Fabric B strips, two of Block 2, and one of Block 1 as shown. Press. Make two and label Rows 4 and 8.

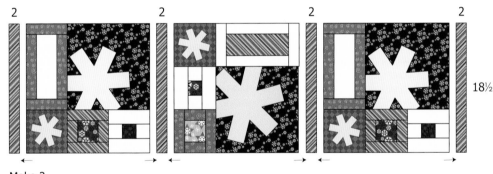

Make 2
Rows 4 & 8

4. Referring to layout on page 105, arrange and sew together rows from steps 1-3 together. Press.

Layering and Finishing

1. Cut backing crosswise into two equal pieces. Sew pieces together lengthwise to make one 80" x 90" (approximate) backing piece. Press and trim to 69" x 90".

2. Referring to Layering the Quilt on page 126, arrange and baste backing, batting, and top together. Hand or machine quilt as desired.

3. Refer to Binding the Quilt on page 126. Sew 2¾" x 42" binding strips end-to-end to make one continuous 2¾"-wide binding strip. Bind quilt to finish.

Snowflake Winter Coverlet
Quick-Fuse Appliqué (page 125)

Tracing Line ————————
Placement Line _.._.._.._.._.._

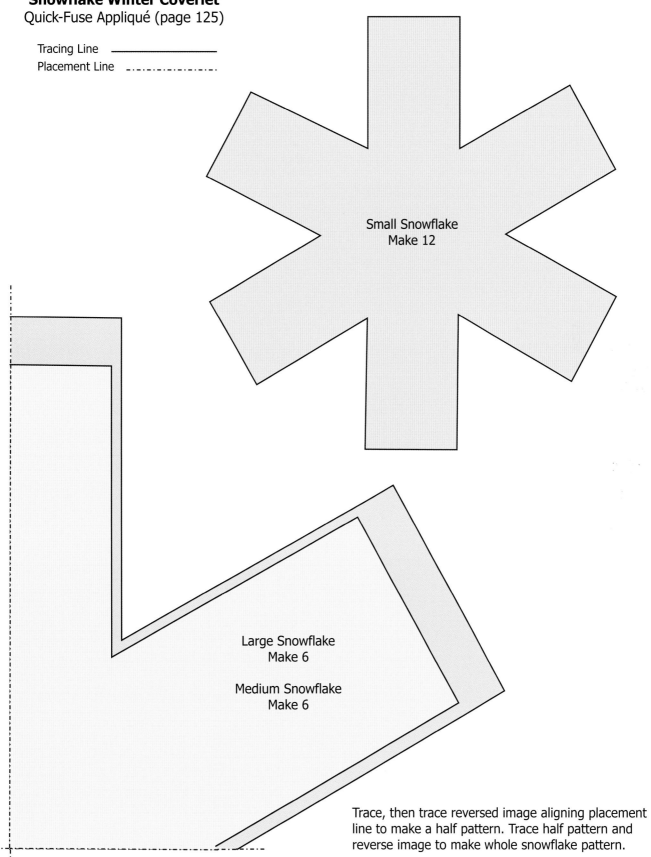

Small Snowflake
Make 12

Large Snowflake
Make 6

Medium Snowflake
Make 6

Trace, then trace reversed image aligning placement line to make a half pattern. Trace half pattern and reverse image to make whole snowflake pattern.

Snowflake Winter
Lap Quilt

Fabric Requirements and Cutting Instructions

Read all instructions before beginning and use ¼"-wide seam allowances throughout. Read Cutting Strips and Pieces on page 124 prior to cutting fabric.

Getting Started
Cuddle up in this smaller version of the coverlet quilt using three blocks of each variation.

Making the Quilt
Refer to Snowflake Winter Coverlet page 103-107 to make this quilt.

1. Refer to Adding the Appliqués page 104, steps 1 and 2 to make three of Unit 1 and three of Unit 2.

2. Refer to steps 3-12 on pages 104-106 to make a three of Block 1 and three of Block 2.

Snowflake Winter *Lap Quilt*

41½" x 61"

Snowflake Winter Lap Quilt Finished Size: 41½" x 61"	FIRST CUT		SECOND CUT	
	Number of Strips or Pieces	Dimensions	Number of Pieces	Dimensions
Fabric A Snowflake Background ¾ yard	2	12½" x 42"	6	12½" squares
Fabric B Unit 3 Center, Unit 6 Border & Sashing ⅞ yard	1 11	3½" x 42" 2" x 42"	3 17 6 6	3½" x 9½" 2" x 18½" 2" x 6½" 2" x 3½"
Fabric C Unit 3 Border, Unit 4 Center, Unit 7 & 8 Borders ⅝ yard Note: See yardage below for snowflake appliqués	1 3 3	3½" x 42" 2½" x 42" 2" x 42"	3 12 12 6 6	3½" x 9½" 2½" x 6½" 2½" squares 2" x 9½" 2" x 6½"
Fabric D Unit 4 & Unit 5 Borders ⅓ yard	4	2" x 42"	6 12 6	2" x 9½" 2" x 6½" 2" x 3½"
Fabric E Unit 5 Center ⅙ yard	1	3½" x 42"	3	3½" squares
Fabric F Unit 6 & Unit 7 Center ⅙ yard	1	3½" x 42"	3 3	3½" squares 2½" squares
Fabric G Unit 8 Center & Sashing Cornerstones ⅛ yard	1	2½" x 42"	3 12	2½" squares 2" squares
Fabric H Accent Square ¼ yard	1	6½" x 42"	6	6½" squares
Binding ⅝ yard	6	2¾" x 42"		
Backing - 2⅔ yards Batting - 48" x 67" Snowflake Appliqués - 1 yard Lightweight Fusible Web (18"-wide) - 2 yards Stabilizer (20"-wide) - 1½ yards				

Assembling and Finishing the Quilt

Refer to layout for steps 1-4.

1. Arrange and sew together three 2" Fabric G squares to two 2" x 18½" Fabric B strips. Press. Make four and label Rows 1, 3, 5, and 7.

2. Arrange and sew together three 2" x 18½" Fabric B strips, one of Block 1, and one of Block 2. Press. Make two and label Rows 2 and 6.

3. Arrange and sew together three 2" x 18½" Fabric B strips, one of Block 2, and one of Block 1. Press. Label Row 4.

4. Arrange and sew rows together. Press.

5. Cut backing crosswise into two equal pieces. Sew pieces together lengthwise to make one 48" x 80" (approximate) backing piece. Press and trim to 48" x 67".

6. Referring to Layering the Quilt on page 126, arrange and baste backing, batting, and top together. Hand or machine quilt as desired.

7. Refer to Binding the Quilt on page 126. Sew 2¾" x 42" binding strips end-to-end to make one continuous 2¾"-wide binding strip. Bind quilt to finish.

Block of the Weekend
Appliqué and Pieced Quilt

2½ DAYS

Weekend Planner

The modern color scheme and bowl shape with simple botanical appliqués puts this wall quilt design at the top of the list as a staff favorite. Four blocks make it the perfect size for a wall quilt; however, make as many blocks as you like to make a larger quilt. Unless you're under a deadline, spread this project across five weekends or divide it up anyway that makes sense for your schedule. Spend a little time each weekend and before you know it your top will be complete.

Weekend One

SATURDAY MORNING

For your first weekend spend a half day planning, coordinating and collecting your fabrics. (Don't forget to check your scrap stash) If you are using it as wall art, take the time to coordinate your colors to the room that it will hang in. The cleaner and simpler that your color story is, the more sophisticated it will be.

SATURDAY AFTERNOON

Plan on about 1½ hours to cut and piece the bowl and background for each of the four blocks. That's it for this weekend!

Weekend Two - Five

Each weekend set aside a couple of hours to cut, fuse, and machine appliqué the appliqué shapes to complete one block each weekend. If you love handwork, consider using embroidery floss and do a buttonhole stitch around the appliqués. Naturally, handwork will take longer, but it keeps your fingers out of the cookie jar.

Weekend Six

For your wrap-up weekend, spend an hour adding the borders.

How long it will take you to accomplish tasks is an estimate and may vary greatly per individual. You may want to allow extra time for any distractions that may come up – like hunting down your seam ripper. *(Happens to the best of us!)*

Block of the Weekend Appliqué & Pieced Quilt Finished Size: 32" x 32"	FIRST CUT		SECOND CUT	
	Number of Strips or Pieces	Dimensions	Number of Pieces	Dimensions
Fabric A Background Fat Quarter each of 4 Fabrics	1* 2* 2*	8½" x 12½" 3½" squares 1½" x 3½" *cut for each fabric		
Fabric B Basket Obese Eighth each of 4 Fabrics	1*	3½" x 42" *cut for each fabric	1*	3½" x 12½"
Fabric C Basket Base ⅛ yard	1	1½" x 42"	4	1½" x 6½"
Fabric D Sashing ½ yard	4 2	2½" x 42" 1½" x 42"	2 2 1 2	2½" x 29½" 2½" x 25½" 1½" x 25½" 1½" x 12½"
Mock Piping ⅙ yard	4	1" x 42"	4	1" x 29½"
First Border ⅙ yard	4	1" x 42"	2 2	1" x 30½" 1" x 29½"
Outside Border ⅙ yard	4	1" x 42"	2 2	1" x 31½" 1" x 30½"
Binding ⅜ yard	4	2¾" x 42"		
Appliqués - Assorted scraps Backing - 1 yard Batting - 36" x 36" Lightweight Fusible Web (18"-wide) - 1 yard Stabilizer (20"-wide) - 1 yard				

Fabric Requirements and Cutting Instructions Read all instructions before beginning and use ¼"-wide seam allowances throughout. Read Cutting Strips and Pieces on page 124 prior to cutting fabric.

Getting Started These flower baskets showcase simple shapes creating unique floral arrangements. Block measures 12½" square (unfinished). Refer to Accurate Seam Allowance on page 124. Whenever possible use Assembly Line Method on page 124. Press seams in direction of arrows.

Assembling the Quilt

1. Refer to Quick Corner Triangles on page 124. Making quick corner triangle units, sew two 3½" Fabric A squares to one 3½" x 12½" Fabric B piece as shown. Press. Make four, one of each combination.

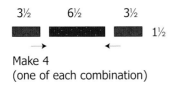

Fabric A = 3½ x 3½
Fabric B= 3½ x 12½
Make 4
(one of each combination)

2. Sew one 1½" x 6½" Fabric C piece between two 1½" x 3½" Fabric A pieces as shown. Press. Make four, one of each combination.

3½   6½   3½

1½

Make 4
(one of each combination)

3. Sew one unit from step 1 between one 8½" x 12½" matching Fabric A piece and one unit from step 2 as shown. Press. Block measures 12½" square.

12½

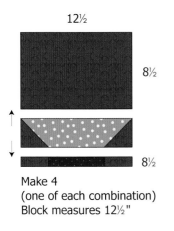

8½

8½

Make 4
(one of each combination)
Block measures 12½"

4. Sew one 1½" x 12½" Fabric D piece between two units from step 3 as shown. Press. Make two.

1½

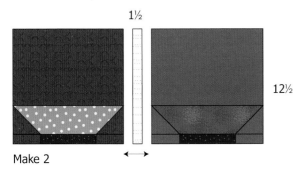

12½

Make 2

Block of the Weekend
Appliqué and Pieced Quilt 32" x 32"

5. Referring to photo on page 109 and layout, sew one 1½" x 25½" Fabric D strip between two units from step 4. Press.

6. Referring to photo on page 109 and layout, sew unit from step 5 between two 2½" x 25½" Fabric D strips. Press seams toward Fabric D. Sew this unit between two 2½" x 29½" Fabric D strips. Press.

7. Fold four 1" x 29½" Mock Piping strips in half wrong sides together to make four ½" x 29½" folded strips. Place two folded strips on quilt top matching top and bottom raw edges. Baste or pin in place. Repeat to baste two folded strips to side edges. Note: Pieces will overlap previous sewn folded strips.

Adding the Appliqués

Refer to appliqué instructions on page 125. Our instructions are for Quick-Fuse Appliqué, but if you prefer hand appliqué, reverse patterns and add ¼"-wide seam allowances.

1. Use patterns on pages 112, 113, 114, and 118 to trace flowers, leaves and circles on paper side of fusible web in quantity noted on each pattern piece. Use appropriate fabrics to prepare all appliqués for fusing.

2. Refer to photo on page 109 and layout to position and fuse appliqués to quilt. Trim stems to match seam lines. Finish appliqué edges with machine satin stitch or other decorative stitching as desired.

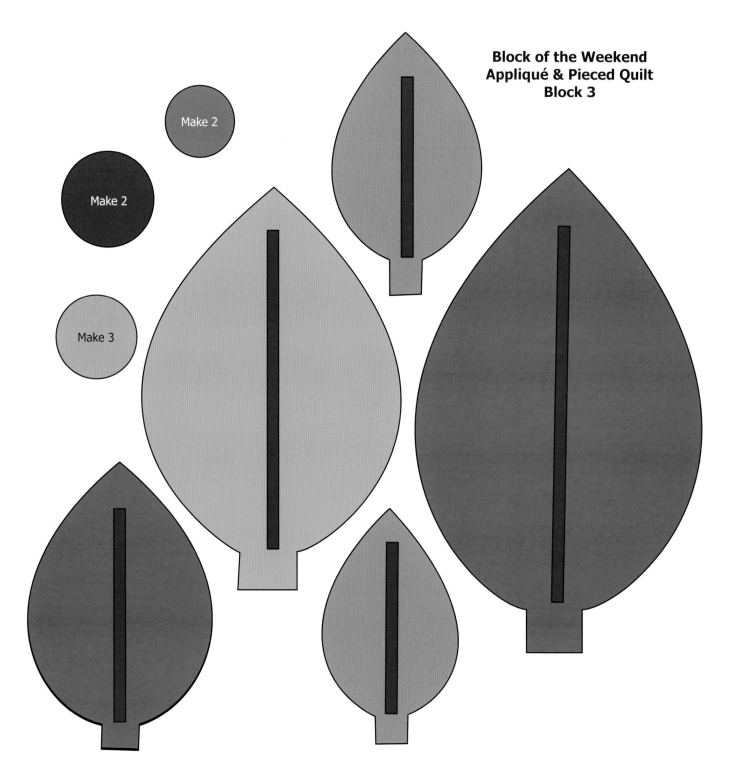

Make 2

Make 2

Make 3

Adding the Borders

1. Refer to Adding the Borders on page 126. Sew 1" x 29½" First Border strips to top and bottom of quilt. Press seams toward border. Sew 1" x 30½" First Border strips to sides of quilt. Press.

2. Sew 1" x 30½" Outside Border strips to top and bottom of quilt. Press seams toward border. Sew 1" x 31½" Outside Border strips to sides of quilt. Press.

Layering and Finishing

1. Referring to Layering the Quilt on page 126, arrange and baste backing, batting, and top together. Hand or machine quilt as desired.

2. Refer to Binding the Quilt on page 126. Use 2¾"-wide binding strips to bind quilt.

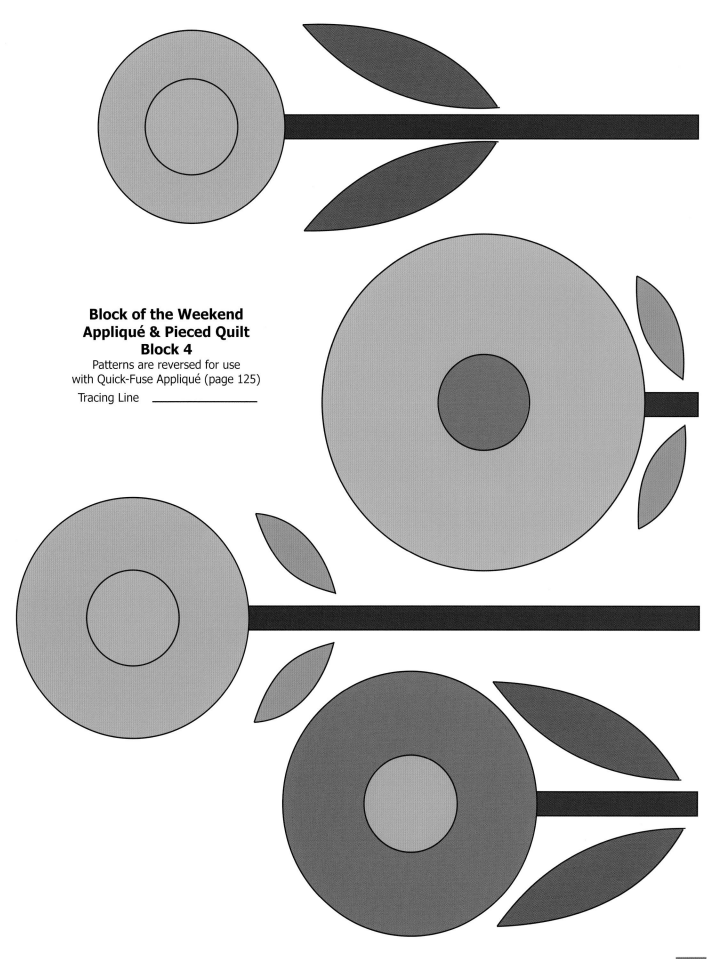

**Block of the Weekend
Appliqué & Pieced Quilt
Block 4**
Patterns are reversed for use
with Quick-Fuse Appliqué (page 125)

Tracing Line —————————

Block of the Weekend
Appliqué & Pieced Quilt
Block 2
Patterns are reversed for use
with Quick-Fuse Appliqué (page 125)
Tracing Line ————————
Tracing Line - - - - - - - - - - - - - - - - -
(will be hidden behind other fabrics)

Simple Statement
Tablerunner

1 DAY

Weekend Planner

● ● ● ● ● ● ● ● ● ● ● ● ●

I love changing up my dining table décor regularly. It's easy to swap it out without making it a major overhaul. Custom made table runners are the perfect solution for doing this. The stripes across the center of this design create the perfect spot to place a simple vase or candles. Choose an appealing fabric for the backing to make the runner reversible.

SATURDAY MORNING

After selecting your seasonal or home décor colors for the runner, you can dig right into this project. In fact, if you have a sewing partner, this might be a fun one to get together and work on. Cutting the pieces and preparing the appliqué shapes will take you around an hour and a half. In another 30 minutes or so you can piece the runner top together.

SATURDAY AFTERNOON

Machine appliquéing the floral design should run you about an hour. This project is petite enough for you to consider doing your own machine quilting. (Of course, hand quilting is always an option too!) If you do decide to tackle this, quilt in the ditch around the appliqué shapes, a 1½" diagonal grid over the stripe center and straight lines spaced 1½" apart over the background. As always your experience level effects how long it takes you to do any part of the process. However, if you are fairly proficient, allow a good 2 to 2½ hours to quilt, add the binding and hand-stitch the binding in place.

How long it will take you to accomplish tasks is an estimate and may vary greatly per individual. You may want to allow extra time for any distractions that may come up – like hunting down your seam ripper. (Happens to the best of us!)

Simple Statement Tablerunner Finished Size: 36" x 13"	FIRST CUT		SECOND CUT	
	Number of Strips or Pieces	Dimensions	Number of Pieces	Dimensions
Fabric A — Background — ½ yard	1 1	12½" x 42" 1½" x 42"	2 1 2	12½" x 13½" 1½" x 12½" 1" x 12½"
Fabric B — Dark Accent — ⅛ yard	2	1" x 42"	6	1" x 12½"
Fabric C — Medium Accent — ⅛ yard	1	1½" x 42"	2	1½" x 12½"
Fabric D — Light Accent — ⅛ yard	2	1" x 42"	4	1" x 12½"
Binding — ⅓ yard	3	2¾" x 42"		

Appliqués - Assorted scraps
Backing - ½ yard
Batting - 40" x 17"
Lightweight Fusible Web (18"-wide) - ½ yard
Stabilizer (20"-wide) - ½ yard

Fabric Requirements and Cutting Instructions
Read all instructions before beginning and use ¼"-wide seam allowances throughout. Read Cutting Strips and Pieces on page 124 prior to cutting fabric.

Getting Started
Graphic flowers take center stage on this tablerunner. Refer to Accurate Seam Allowance on page 124. Whenever possible use Assembly Line Method on page 124. Press seams in direction of arrows.

Making the Tablerunner

1. Arrange and sew together two 1" x 12½" Fabric A pieces, four 1" x 12½" Fabric D pieces, six 1" x 12½" Fabric B pieces, two 12½" x 13½" Fabric A pieces, two 1½" x 12½" Fabric C pieces, and one 1½" x 12½" Fabric A piece as shown. Press.

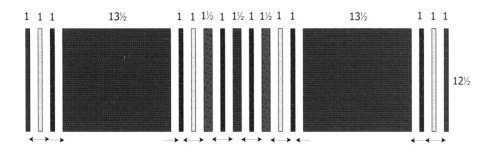

Adding the Appliqués

Refer to appliqué instructions on page 125. Our instructions are for Quick-Fuse Appliqué, but if you prefer hand appliqué, add ¼"-wide seam allowances.

1. Use patterns on page 118 to trace six each of large and small circles, six stems, four large leaves, four medium leaves, and four small leaves on paper side of fusible web. Use appropriate fabrics to prepare all appliqués for fusing.

2. Referring to photo on page 115 and layout below, position and fuse appliqués to quilt. Trim stem ends to match seam lines. Finish appliqué edges with machine satin stitch or other decorative stitching as desired.

Layering and Finishing

1. Referring to Layering the Quilt on page 126, arrange and baste backing, batting, and top together. Hand or machine quilt as desired.

2. Refer to Binding the Quilt on page 126. Use 2¾"-wide binding strips to bind quilt.

Simple Statement *Tablerunner*
36" x 13"

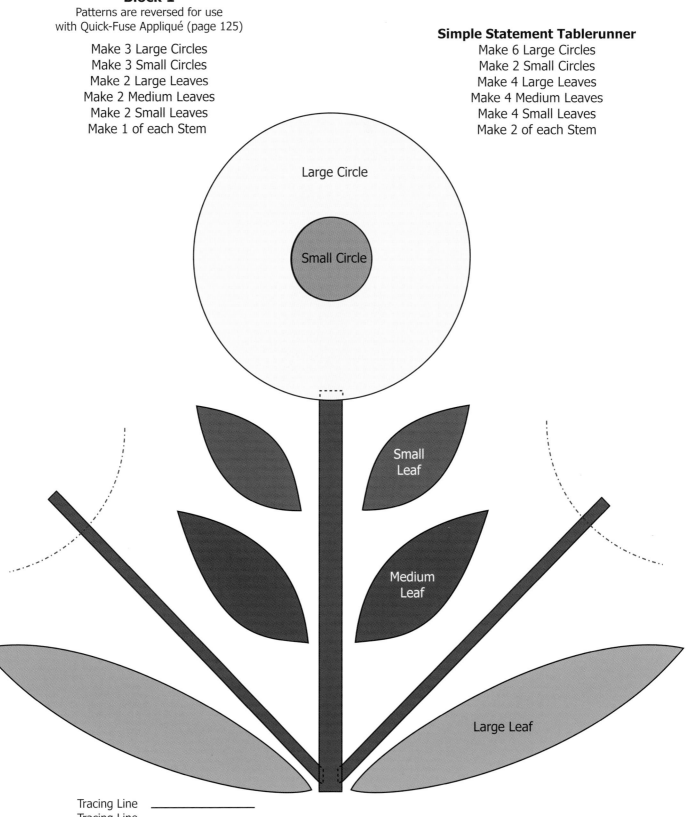

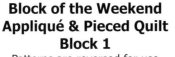

Block of the Weekend
Appliqué & Pieced Quilt
Block 1
Patterns are reversed for use
with Quick-Fuse Appliqué (page 125)

Make 3 Large Circles
Make 3 Small Circles
Make 2 Large Leaves
Make 2 Medium Leaves
Make 2 Small Leaves
Make 1 of each Stem

Simple Statement Tablerunner
Make 6 Large Circles
Make 2 Small Circles
Make 4 Large Leaves
Make 4 Medium Leaves
Make 4 Small Leaves
Make 2 of each Stem

Large Circle

Small Circle

Small Leaf

Medium Leaf

Large Leaf

Tracing Line ———————
Tracing Line - - - - - - - - - - - -
(will be hidden behind other fabrics)
Placement Line - · - · - · - · - · -

Contemporary Classic
Throw Pillows

1 DAY

Weekend Planner

Pillows always add personality and depending on the fabrics and colors you pick, they will reflect your own personal style!

SATURDAY

Small projects like pillows are also satisfying to make because in one short weekend day you can stitch up this stylish pair from start to finish. Cutting and piecing both will take you little more than an hour. Allow yourself a couple of hours to prep and stitch your appliqué pieces. When doing your machine appliqué, the zigzag stitch takes less than half the time of a satin stitch! Quilting is not necessary for pillows, but I sure think it adds a lot of interesting visual texture. In the next hour and a half, machine quilt around the appliqué shapes and straight lines in the background. Your last hour will be spent sewing the backing and inserting the pillow form.

Making Pillow Forms

Make your pillow forms fit your custom pillows perfectly by stitching and stuffing your own. In less than an hour, you'll have them both turned out. I like to use batting instead of muslin to create the forms because you don't see the uneven bumps of the filling that can sometimes show through muslin.

How long it will take you to accomplish tasks is an estimate and may vary greatly per individual. You may want to allow extra time for any distractions that may come up – like hunting down your seam ripper. (Happens to the best of us!)

Fabric Requirements and Cutting Instructions

Read all instructions before beginning and use ¼"-wide seam allowances throughout. Read Cutting Strips and Pieces on page 124 prior to cutting fabric.

Getting Started
These contemporary botanical pillows make great accents for family rooms and bedrooms. Refer to Accurate Seam Allowance on page 124. Whenever possible use Assembly Line Method on page 124. Press seams in direction of arrows.

Contemporary Classic Throw Pillow #1 Finished Size: 18" square	FIRST CUT		SECOND CUT	
	Number of Strips or Pieces	Dimensions	Number of Pieces	Dimensions
Fabric A Background Fat Quarter	1	12½" square		
Fabric B First Border ⅛ yard	2	1½" x 42"	2 2	1½" x 14½" 1½" x 12½"
Fabric C Second Border ⅛ yard	2	1½" x 42"	2 2	1½" x 16½" 1½" x 14½"
Fabric D Outside Border ⅛ yard	2	1½" x 42"	2 2	1½" x 18½" 1½" x 16½"
Backing ½ yard	1	12" x 42"	2	12" x 18½"

Appliqués - Assorted scraps
Lining - ⅝ yard (does not show)
Batting - 22" x 22"
Lightweight Fusible Web (18"-wide) - ¼ yard
Stabilizer (20"-wide) - ¼ yard
18" Pillow Form

Making Pillow #1 Top

1. Sew 12½" Fabric A square between two 1½" x 12½" Fabric B pieces. Press seams toward Fabric B. Sew this unit between two 1½" x 14½" Fabric B strips as shown in step 3 diagram. Press.

2. Sew unit from step 1 between two 1½" x 14½" Fabric C strips. Press seams toward Fabric C. Sew this unit between two 1½" x 16½" Fabric C strips as shown in step 3 diagram. Press.

3. Sew unit from step 2 between two 1½" x 16½" Fabric D strips. Press seams toward Fabric D. Sew this unit between two 1½" x 18½" Fabric D strips as shown. Press.

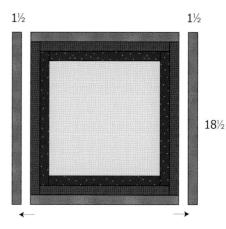

Making Pillow #2 Top

1. Fold two 1" x 9½" Fabric B pieces in half wrong sides together to make two ½" x 9½" folded pieces. Place each folded piece on 9½" x 11½" Fabric A piece, matching raw edges. Baste or pin in place. Sew this unit between two 1" x 9½" Fabric C pieces as shown. Press.

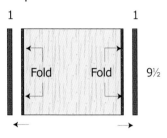

2. Sew unit from step 1 between two 2" x 9½" Fabric D pieces as shown. Press.

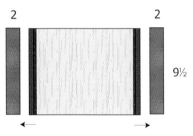

Adding the Appliqués

Refer to appliqué instructions on page 125. Our instructions are for Quick-Fuse Appliqué, but if you prefer hand appliqué, reverse patterns and add ¼"-wide seam allowances.

1. Use patterns on pages 122 and 123 to trace leaves and circles on paper side of fusible web noting quantity needed on pattern pieces. Use appropriate fabrics to prepare all appliqués for fusing.

2. Refer to photo on page 119 and layout to position and fuse appliqués to pillow tops. Finish appliqué edges with machine satin stitch or other decorative stitching as desired.

Contemporary Classic Throw Pillow #2 Finished Size: 9" x 15"	FIRST CUT		SECOND CUT	
	Number of Strips or Pieces	Dimensions	Number of Pieces	Dimensions
Fabric A Background Fat Quarter	1	9½" x 11½"		
Fabric B Mock Piping ⅛ yard	1	1" x 42"	2	1" x 9½"
Fabric C Accent Border ⅛ yard	1	1" x 42"	2	1" x 9½"
Fabric D Outside Border ⅛ yard	1	2" x 42"	2	2" x 9½"
Backing ⅓ yard	1	9½" x 42"	2	9½" x 10½"

Appliqués - Assorted scraps
Lining - ⅜ yard (does not show)
Batting - 13" x 19"
Lightweight Fusible Web (18"-wide) - ¼ yard
Stabilizer (20"-wide) - ¼ yard
9" x 15" Pillow Form

Pillow General Instructions

1. Refer to Finishing Pillows on page 127, step 1, to prepare pillow top for quilting. Quilt as desired.

2. For Pillow #1, use two 12" x 18½" Backing pieces to finish pillow. For Pillow #2, use two 9½" x 11½" backing pieces to finish pillow. Refer to Finishing Pillows, page 127, steps 2-4, to sew backing.

3. Insert 18" pillow form for Pillow #1. Insert 9" x 15" pillow form for Pillow #2. Optional: Refer to Pillow Forms page 127 to make pillow forms if desired. Pillow #1 uses two 18½" squares of fabric and Pillow #2 uses two 9½" x 15½" fabric pieces.

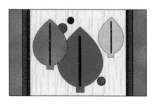

Pillow #1
18" square

Pillow #2
9" x 15"

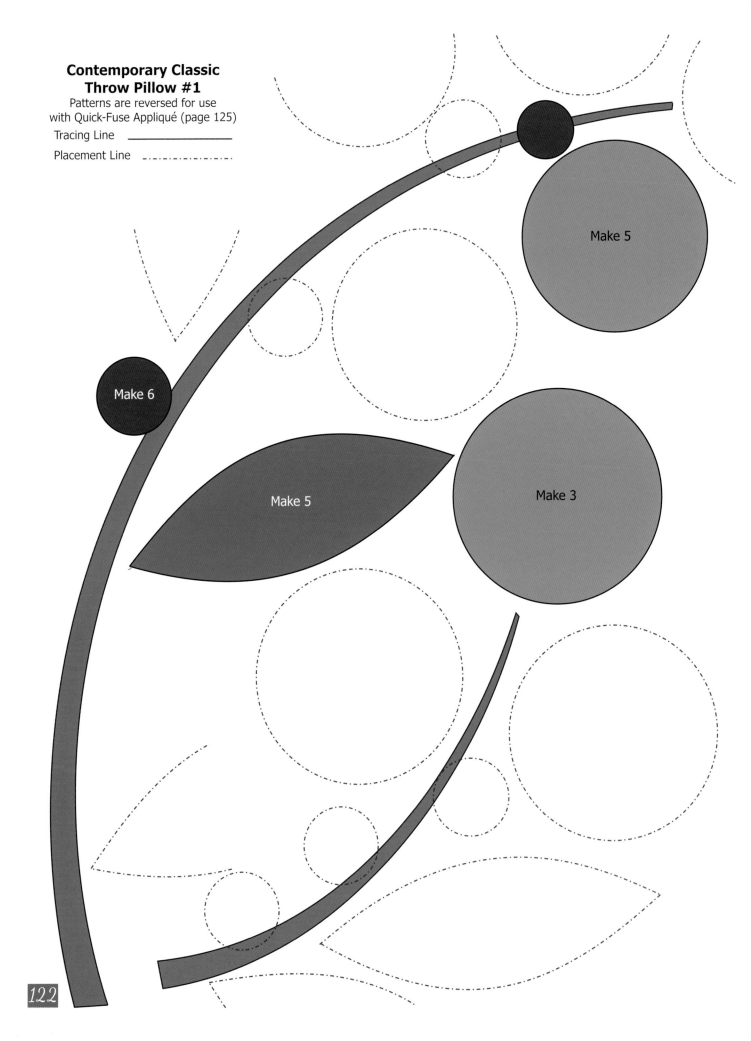

Contemporary Classic
Throw Pillow #1
Patterns are reversed for use
with Quick-Fuse Appliqué (page 125)

Tracing Line _____

Placement Line ·—··—··—··—·

Make 5

Make 6

Make 5

Make 3

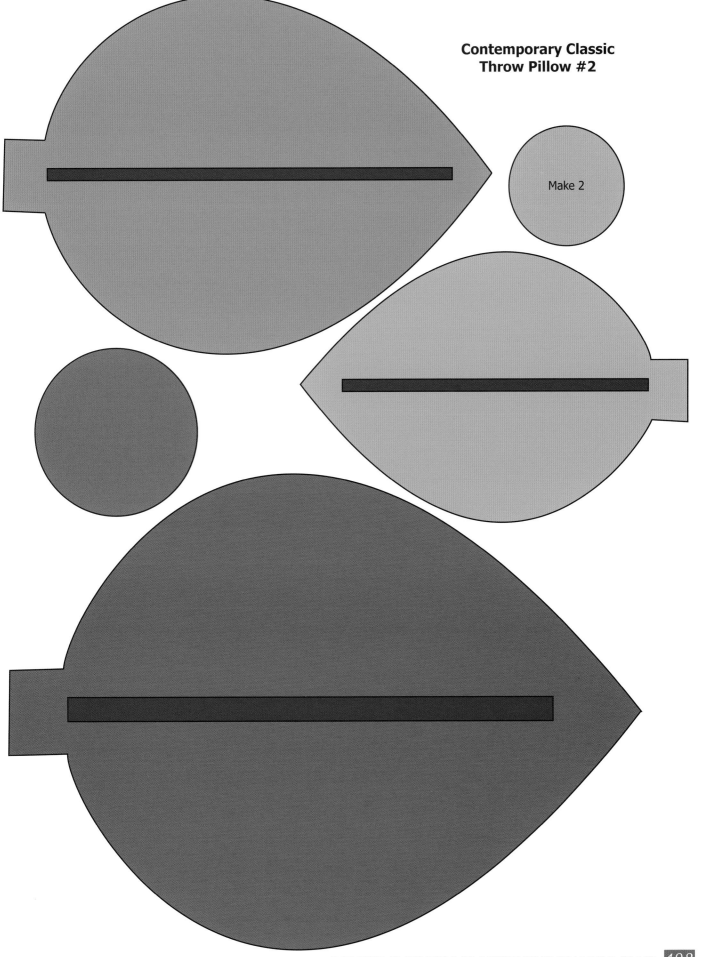

**Contemporary Classic
Throw Pillow #2**

Make 2

General Directions

Cutting Strips and Pieces

We recommend washing cotton fabrics in cold water and pressing before making projects in this book. Using a rotary cutter, see-through ruler, and a cutting mat, cut the strips and pieces for the project. If indicated on the Cutting Chart, some will need to be cut again into smaller strips and pieces. Make second cuts in order shown to maximize use of fabric. The yardage amounts are based on an approximate fabric width of 42" and Fat Quarters are based on 18" x 22" pieces.

Pressing

Pressing is very important for accurate seam allowances. Press seams using either steam or dry heat with an "up and down" motion. Do not use side-to-side motion as this will distort the unit or block. Set the seam by pressing along the line of stitching, then press seams to one side as indicated by project instructions and diagram arrows.

Twisting Seams

When a block has several seams meeting in the center as shown, there will be less bulk if seam allowances are pressed in a circular direction and the center intersection "twisted". Remove 1-2 stitches in the seam allowance to enable the center to twist and lay flat. This technique aids in quilt assembly by allowing the seams to fall opposite each other when repeated blocks are next to each other. The technique works well with 4-patch blocks, pinwheel blocks, and quarter-square triangle blocks.

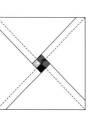

Accurate Seam Allowance

Accurate seam allowances are always important, but especially when the blocks contain many pieces and the quilt top contains multiple pieced borders. If each seam is off as little as ¹⁄₁₆", you'll soon find yourself struggling with components that just won't fit.

To ensure seams are a perfect ¼"-wide, try this simple test: Cut three strips of fabric, each exactly 1½" x 12". With right sides together, and long raw edges aligned, sew two strips together, carefully maintaining a ¼" seam. Press seam to one side. Add the third strip to complete the strip set. Press and measure. The finished strip set should measure 3½" x 12". The center strip should measure 1"-wide, the two outside strips 1¼"-wide, and the seam allowances exactly ¼".

If your measurements differ, check to make sure that seams have been pressed flat. If strip set still doesn't "measure up," try stitching a new strip set, adjusting the seam allowance until a perfect ¼"-wide seam is achieved.

Assembly Line Method

Whenever possible, use an assembly line method. Position pieces right sides together and line up next to sewing machine. Stitch first unit together, then continue sewing others without cutting threads. When all units are sewn, clip threads to separate. Press seams in direction of arrows as shown in step-by-step project diagrams.

Quick Corner Triangles

Quick corner triangles are formed by simply sewing fabric squares to other squares or rectangles. The directions and diagrams with each project illustrate what size pieces to use and where to place squares on the corresponding piece. Follow steps 1–3 below to make quick corner triangle units.

1. With pencil and ruler, draw diagonal line on wrong side of fabric square that will form the triangle. This will be your sewing line.

Sewing line

2. With right sides together, place square on corresponding piece. Matching raw edges, pin in place, and sew ON drawn line. Trim off excess fabric, leaving ¼"-wide seam allowance as shown.

Trim ¼" away from sewing line

3. Press seam in direction of arrow as shown in step-by-step project diagram. Measure completed quick corner triangle unit to ensure the greatest accuracy.

Finished quick corner triangle unit

Fussy Cut

To make a "fussy cut," carefully position ruler or template over a selected design in fabric. Include seam allowances before cutting desired pieces.

Quick-Fuse Appliqué

Quick-fuse appliqué is a method of adhering appliqué pieces to a background with fusible web. For quick and easy results, simply quick-fuse appliqué pieces in place. Use sewable, lightweight fusible web for the projects in this book unless otherwise indicated. Finish raw edges with stitching as desired. Laundering is not recommended unless edges are finished.

1. With paper side up, lay fusible web over appliqué pattern. Leaving ½" space between pieces, trace all elements of design. Cut around traced pieces, approximately ¼" outside traced line.

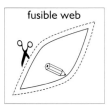

2. With paper side up, position and press fusible web to wrong side of selected fabrics. Follow manufacturer's directions for iron temperature and fusing time. Cut out each piece on traced line.

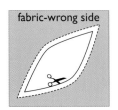

3. Remove paper backing from pieces. A thin film will remain on wrong side of fabric. Position and fuse all pieces of one appliqué design at a time onto background, referring to photos and diagrams for placement. Fused design will be the reverse of traced pattern.

Appliqué Pressing Sheet

An appliqué pressing sheet is very helpful when there are many small elements to apply using a quick-fuse appliqué technique. The pressing sheet allows small items to be bonded together before applying them to the background. The sheet is coated with a special material that prevents fusible web from adhering permanently to the sheet. Follow manufacturer's directions. Remember to let fabric cool completely before lifting it from the appliqué sheet. If not cooled, the fusible web could remain on the sheet instead of on the fabric.

For accurate layout, place a line drawing of finished project under pressing sheet. Use this as a guide to adhere pieces.

Machine Appliqué

This technique should be used when you are planning to launder quick-fuse projects. Several different stitches can be used: small narrow zigzag stitch, satin stitch, blanket stitch, or another decorative machine stitch. Use an open toe appliqué foot if your machine has one. Use a stabilizer to obtain even stitches and help prevent puckering. Always practice first to check machine settings.

1. Fuse all pieces following Quick-Fuse Appliqué directions.

2. Cut a piece of stabilizer large enough to extend beyond the area to be stitched. Pin to the wrong side of fabric.

3. Select thread to match appliqué.

4. Following the order that appliqués were positioned, stitch along the edges of each section. Anchor beginning and ending stitches by tying off or stitching in place two or three times.

5. Complete all stitching, then remove stabilizer.

Hand Appliqué

Hand appliqué is easy when you start out with the right supplies. Cotton and machine embroidery thread are easy to work with. Pick a color that matches the appliqué fabric as closely as possible. Use appliqué or silk pins for holding shapes in place and a long, thin needle, such as a sharp, for stitching.

1. Make a template for every shape in the appliqué design. Use a dotted line to show where pieces overlap.

2. Place template on right side of appliqué fabric. Trace around template.

3. Cut out shapes ¼" beyond traced line.

4. Position shapes on background fabric, referring to quilt layout. Pin shapes in place.

5. When layering and stitching appliqué shapes, always work from background to foreground. Where shapes overlap, do not turn under and stitch edges of bottom pieces. Turn and stitch the edges of the piece on top.

6. Use the traced line as your turn-under guide. Entering from the wrong side of the appliqué shape, bring the needle up on the traced line. Using the tip of the needle, turn under the fabric along the traced line. Using blind stitch, stitch along folded edge to join the appliqué shape to the background fabric. Turn under and stitch about ¼" at a time.

Adding the Borders

1. Measure quilt through the center from side to side. Trim two border strips to this measurement. Sew to top and bottom of quilt. Press seams toward border.

2. Measure quilt through the center from top to bottom, including borders added in step 1. Trim border strips to this measurement. Sew to sides and press. Repeat to add additional borders.

Layering the Quilt

1. Cut backing and batting 4" to 8" larger than quilt top.

2. Lay pressed backing on bottom (right side down), batting in middle, and pressed quilt top (right side up) on top. Make sure everything is centered and that backing and batting are flat. Backing and batting will extend beyond quilt top.

3. Begin basting in center and work toward outside edges. Baste vertically and horizontally, forming a 3"–4" grid. Baste or pin completely around edge of quilt top. Quilt as desired. Remove basting.

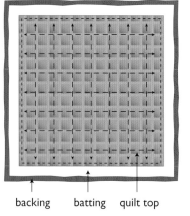

backing   batting   quilt top

Binding the Quilt

1. Trim batting and backing to ¼" beyond raw edge of quilt top. This will add fullness to binding.

2. Join binding strips to make one continuous strip if needed. To join, place 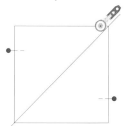 strips perpendicular to each other, right sides together, and draw a diagonal line. Sew on drawn line and trim triangle extensions, leaving a ¼"-wide seam allowance. Continue stitching ends together to make the desired length. Press seams open.

3. Fold and press binding strips in half lengthwise with wrong sides together.

4. Measure quilt through center from side to side. Cut two binding strips to this measurement. Lay binding strips on top and bottom edges of quilt top with raw edges of binding and quilt top aligned. Sew through all layers, ¼" from quilt edge. Press binding away from quilt top.

Front of Quilt

5. Measure quilt through center from top to bottom, including binding just added. Cut two binding strips to this measurement and sew to sides through all layers, including binding just added. Press.

6. Folding top and bottom first, fold binding around to back then repeat with sides. Press and pin in position. Hand-stitch binding in place using a blind stitch.

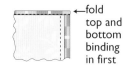

←fold top and bottom binding in first

Making Bias Strips

1. Refer to Fabric Requirements and Cutting Instructions for the amount of fabric required for the specific bias needed.

2. Remove selvages from the fabric piece and cut into a square. Mark edge with straight pin where selvages were removed as shown. Cut square once diagonally into two equal 45° triangles. (For larger squares, fold square in half diagonally and gently press fold. Open fabric square and cut on fold.)

3. Place pinned edges right sides together and stitch along edge with a ¼" seam. Press seam open.

4. Using a ruler and rotary cutter, cut bias strips to width specified in quilt directions.

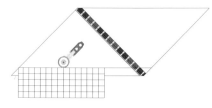

5. Each strip has a diagonal end. To join, place strips perpendicular to each other, right sides together, matching diagonal cut edges and allowing tips of angles to extend approximately ¼" beyond edges. Sew ¼"-wide seams. Continue stitching ends together to make the desired length. Press seams open. Follow Binding the Quilt steps 3-6 to cut and sew binding to quilt.

Mitered Borders

A mitered border is usually "fussy cut" to highlight a motif or design. Borders are cut slightly longer than needed to allow for centering of motif or matching corners.

1. Cut the border strips or strip sets as indicated for quilt.

2. Measure each side of the quilt and mark center with a pin. Fold each border strip in half crosswise to find its midpoint and mark with a pin. Using the side measurements, measure out from the midpoint and place a pin to show where the edges of the quilt will be.

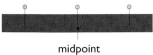
midpoint

3. Align a border strip to quilt. Pin at midpoints and pin-marked ends first, then along entire side, easing to fit if necessary.

4. Sew border to quilt, stopping and starting ¼" from pin-marked end points. Repeat to sew all four border strips to quilt.

quilt front

5. Fold corner of quilt diagonally, right sides together, matching seams and borders. Place a long ruler along fold line extending across border. Draw a diagonal line across border from fold to edge of border. This is the stitching line. Starting at ¼" mark, stitch on drawn line. Check for squareness, then trim excess. Press seam open.

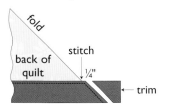
fold
back of quilt
stitch
¼"
trim

Finishing Pillows

Any block in this book or combination of blocks can be made into an accent pillow. To determine the backing piece size needed, measure unfinished pillow top width and length. Divide the width measurement by two, and add 2¾" to this measurement. Cut two pieces of backing fabric to the new width measurement by the length measurement and follow directions below to complete pillow.

1. Layer batting between pillow top and lining. Baste. Hand or machine quilt as desired. Trim batting and lining even with raw edge of pillow top.

2. Narrow hem one long edge of each backing piece by folding under ¼" to wrong side. Press. Fold under ¼" again to wrong side. Press. Stitch along folded edge.

Circle Template
Trace four times aligning placement lines to make a whole circle.

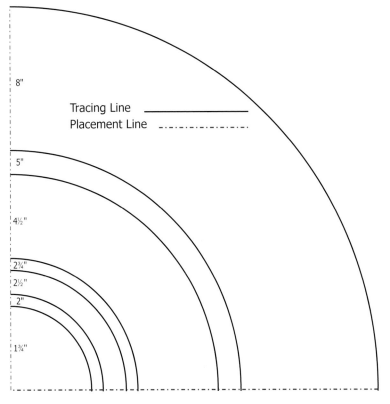

8"
5"
4½"
2¾"
2½"
2"
1¾"

Tracing Line ——————
Placement Line ·—·—·—·—·—·

3. With sides up, lay one backing piece over second piece so hemmed edges overlap, making backing unit the same measurement as the pillow top. Baste backing pieces together at top and bottom where they overlap.

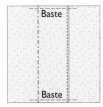
Baste
Baste

4. With right sides together, position and pin pillow top to backing. Using ¼"-wide seam, sew around edges, trim corners, turn right side out, and press.

Pillow Forms

Cut two pieces of fabric ½" larger than finished pillow size. Place right sides together, aligning raw edges. Using ¼"-wide seam, sew around all edges, leaving 5" opening for turning. Trim corners and turn right side out. Stuff to desired fullness with polyester fiberfill and hand-stitch opening closed.

About Debbie

A talented designer, author, and entrepreneur, Debbie Mumm has been creating charming artwork and quilt designs for twenty five years.

Debbie got her start in the quilting industry in 1986 with her unique and simple-to-construct quilt patterns. Since that time, she has authored more than sixty books featuring quilting and home decorating projects and has led her business to become a multi-faceted enterprise that includes publishing, fabric design, and licensed art divisions.

Known world-wide for the many licensed products that feature her designs, Debbie loves to bring traditional elements together with fresh palettes and modern themes to create the look of today's country.

Designs by Debbie Mumm

Special thanks to my creative teams:

Editorial & Project Design

Debbie Mumm: Managing Editor & Designer
Nancy Kirkland: Quilt Designer/Seamstress
Georgie Gerl: Technical Writer/Editor
Ellen Pahl: Technical Editor
Anita Pederson: Machine Quilter

Book Design & Production

Monica Ziegler: Graphic Designer

Photography

Tom Harlow
Carolyn Ogden: Photo Stylist
Debbie Mumm: Photo Stylist

Discover More from Debbie Mumm®

Debbie Mumm's®
25 Years of Quilts
128-page, soft cover

Fresh Cuts
by Debbie Mumm®
112-page, soft cover

Debbie Mumm's®
Quick Quilts for Home
112-page, soft cover

Debbie Mumm's®
I Care with Quilts
96-page, soft cover

Produced by:
Debbie Mumm, Inc.
1015 N Calispel Street
Suite A
Spokane, WA 99201
(509) 466-3572
Fax (509) 466-6919

www.debbiemumm.com

Published by:
Leisure Arts, Inc
5701 Ranch Drive
Little Rock, AR • 72223
www.leisurearts.com

Available at local fabric and craft shops or at
debbiemumm.com